CRITICAL

D0346653

NEWCASTLE-UNDER-LYME
COLLEGE LIBRARY

How To Books for Students

Critical Thinking for Students
Getting a Job after University
Going to University
Know Your Rights: Students
Know Your Rights: Teachers
Master Book-Keeping
Mastering Business English
Master GCSE Accounts
Master Languages
Pass Exams Without Anxiety
Pass That Interview
Research Methods
Spend a Year Abroad
Study Abroad

Study & Learn
Study & Live In Britain
Studying at University
Studying for a Degree
Survive at College
Taking In Students
Taking Your A-Levels
Use a Library
Write a Report
Write an Assignment
Write Your Dissertation
Writing an Essay
Writing Business Letters

Other titles in preparation

The How To Series now contains more than 150 titles in the following categories:

Business Basics
Family Reference
Jobs & Careers
Living & Working Abroad
Student Handbooks
Successful Writing

Please send for a free copy of the latest catalogue for full details (see back cover for address).

CRITICAL THINKING FOR STUDENTS

How to use your recommended texts
on a college or university course

Roy van den Brink-Budgen

How To Books

Cartoons by Mike Flanagan

British Library Cataloguing in Publication Data

A catalogue record for this book is available from the British Library.

© Copyright 1996 by Roy van den Brink-Budgen.

First published in 1996 by How To Books Ltd, Plymbridge House, Estover Road, Plymouth PL6 7PZ, United Kingdom. Tel: Plymouth (01752) 202301. Fax: (01752) 202331.

Note: The material contained in this book is set out in good faith for general guidance and no liability can be accepted for loss or expense incurred as a result of relying in particular circumstances on statements made in this book. The laws and regulations are complex and liable to change, and readers should check the current position with the relevant authorities before making personal arrangements.

Produced for How To Books by Deer Park Productions.
Typeset by Concept Communications (Design & Print) Ltd, Crayford, Kent.
Printed and bound by Cromwell Press, Broughton Gifford, Melksham, Wiltshire.

Contents

5

Preface

Much attention has been given recently to the subject of 'thinking skills' or 'core skills'. The idea behind this emphasis on such skills is that, whatever the specific subject you are studying, you are going to be using skills which are common to many subjects. So, if you can develop and improve these skills, then your performance in the subjects you are studying should also be developed and improved.

The aim of this book is to introduce you to one of these 'core skills', **critical thinking**. This is concerned with arguments, with ways in which people try to show that their case is better than someone else's. It is hoped that the book will enable you to make useful assessments of such arguments, whether you meet them in a text-book or newspaper, on the television or in the bar. The book will also help you to produce better arguments of your own, whether this is for an essay, a report, a paper, for a debate or a discussion. It should also make you much more confident in handling material that you are expected to read, by helping you to pick out the main points and to assess them.

This book does not regard the subject of critical thinking as an end in itself, as something which you should study for its own sake. This book sees critical thinking as having a place in education only if it earns its keep, as contributing to an improved educational performance. Hopefully, it will earn its keep by doing that for you.

Each chapter provides a number of examples which illustrate what is being shown. In addition, each chapter provides exercises for you to try out your developing skills. Both examples and exercises are written in a way that makes them approachable and hopefully interesting. The subjects used are often of topical concern, such as pollution, animal rights and crime.

I should like to thank my children – Simon, Petra, Ruth, Adam and Roy – for their tolerance of my argumentative nature. But, in particular, I should like to thank Annie, my wife, for all her reasoning on my behalf, all her reassurances that things were going well when I thought they weren't, and for being a splendid argument for the state of marriage.

Roy van den Brink-Budgen

IS THIS YOU?

University candidate   Sixthform student

Essay writer

Undergraduate   College student

Postgraduate

Finals candidate   Studying education

Writing a dissertation

OU student   Mature student

Part-time student

Tutor   Student supervisor

Lecturer

Doing a project   Report writer

Returning to study

Debater   Foreign student

Distance learner

Studying science/technology   Planning research

Preparing for a higher degree

Revising rusty techniques   Social scientist

1
Identifying Arguments

PERSUADING AND ARGUING

If you were asked to say what is meant by an 'argument', you would probably use words like 'disagreement' and 'dispute'. The following example would fit with this description:

> I can't understand people who say that smokers shouldn't be allowed to smoke in public places. I think anyone should be allowed to smoke anywhere.

In this example, the speaker expresses a clear disagreement. Their argument is with those who want to restrict the rights of smokers. You can come up with all sorts of other examples, ranging from simple disagreements between friends to much more complex ones like those between political parties.

However, in critical thinking, the meaning of the word 'argument' goes further than just 'disagreement'. It is not enough to disagree: there must be an attempt to persuade someone that one position is preferable to another. Looking back at our first example, how does the speaker try to persuade us that 'anyone should be allowed to smoke anywhere'?

The answer is simple: they don't.

Persuading with reasons

The speaker in the first example did no more than disagree with those who think that smoking should not be allowed in public places. Nothing in what was said would have changed your mind on the subject. However, look at the next example:

> People should be allowed to smoke anywhere. Smoking's not illegal, and millions of people get huge pleasure from it.

What's the difference? As you will have seen, the speaker has now given us two reasons why 'people should be allowed to smoke anywhere'. The first is that smoking isn't illegal; the second is that millions of people enjoy it. Whether or not you agree with these reasons, the point remains that this second example is an attempt to be **persuasive**. It's an attempt to get beyond simple disagreement.

It also calls out for an answer. It would not be enough to reply that you disagree. Even if you are not persuaded, the reasons have to be at least acknowledged. In responding to this argument, you would have to respond with your own reasons. In other words, an argument has to be answered with an argument.

So what have we established so far?

● Arguments have reasons.
● Arguments are meant to be persuasive.

You can see then that arguments for the critical thinker are not like arm-twisting attempts to make other people accept a particular position. They are not bullying orders to see things one way rather than another. Instead, they set up reasons in such a way that, if you accept those reasons, you are likely to be persuaded of a particular position.

Concluding from reasons

Look again at our second example. What is the function of the first sentence?

As we have seen, this is what the speaker wants to persuade us to accept. It is, if you like, the main point of what is being said. It is what we call the **conclusion** of the argument.

We usually think of a 'conclusion' as something that comes at the end. For example, we talk about the concluding part of a television series. But when we use the word 'conclusion' in critical thinking, we are using it in a specific way. We are not using it to mean the final sentence in a passage, in that, though the conclusion of an argument might well be placed at the end of it, it does not have to be. It can come anywhere – even, as in the second example above, at the beginning. But, unless a conclusion is drawn, an argument has not been created. The reasons must be going somewhere: there must be an attempt to persuade us of something.

It is this feature of an argument, that reasons must be going somewhere, that returns us to the familiar meaning of 'conclusion' as 'end'. Even if the conclusion of an argument need not literally be placed at its end, it is where an argument 'ends up' by being what it tries to establish.

We can now add another feature of arguments.

● Arguments always have a conclusion.

By now, you will probably have a few questions which need answering. It would be useful to answer them before we move on.

Questions and answers

How will I know when I am dealing with an argument?

You will need to find at least one part which acts as a reason for a conclusion and, of course, a conclusion itself.

How will I be able to tell what is a reason and what is a conclusion?

The simplest way of distinguishing between the two is to consider what the function of each is. The conclusion is the main purpose of the argument, expressing what the arguer wants to persuade others to accept. A reason will support this conclusion, literally giving a reason why we should accept it.

How many reasons does an argument have to have?

An argument must have a minimum of one reason. Beyond that, there is not limit to the number.

*You have said that arguments are attempts to persuade others of a particular position. What if they don't persuade others? Do arguments **have** to persuade in order to be called arguments?*

As long as there is at least one reason supporting a conclusion, there is an argument. Even if it's a very poor argument – one which is unlikely to (and shouldn't) persuade anybody – it's an argument nonetheless.

So if arguments are intended to persuade others, are all attempts to persuade others called arguments?

No. There are many examples of attempts to persuade which are not arguments. For example, advertisers sometimes try to sell a product (try to persuade us to buy) by using no words at all. Put simply, if you've found an argument, it'll be an attempt to be persuasive; but if you've found something which attempts to be persuasive, it need not be an argument.

FINDING ARGUMENTS

Now that you know that arguments contain reasons and conclusions, you know what to look for. As we said above, a reason will in some way support a conclusion. You will remember our example about smoking in public places. If we change the wording slightly and turn it round to emphasise the conclusion, you'll be able to see how the reasons do their work:

> Smoking's not illegal. In addition, millions of people get huge pleasure from it. Therefore people should be allowed to smoke anywhere.

Looking for words as clues

In this version the conclusion is flagged by the word 'therefore'. Very often some sort of word like this will alert you to where the conclusion is. Other words include 'so', 'then', 'thus' and 'in consequence'. Put any of these words in place of 'therefore' and you will see how they do the same job. You will also find, as in the above example, that a word like 'should' will often give you a clue that a conclusion might have been drawn (another is 'must'). However, conclusions are not always helpfully flagged in this way. In our original version of the smoking example, no such word was there, even though a conclusion was still being drawn. This means that, to be an effective critical thinker, you need to be able to find conclusions without using word clues.

There will be no such helpful word clues to indicate the presence of reasons. Again, you will have to do some work to establish whether or not reasons have been provided. This is where knowing the function of reasons will help you.

Exercises in finding arguments

Introduction

Now that you know something of arguments, it will be useful to practise your skill at identifying them. Read the following short passages and work out which are arguments and which are not. Remember that you are looking for passages which contain reasons supporting a conclusion. To help you get along, we start with an example. Is this an argument?

> Unless people invest in computers for their home, they are going to be left behind in the huge technological changes affecting our lives. Computers have become so much cheaper than they used to be. Most children feel entirely comfortable with them.

This is not an argument. Whichever order you put these three sentences in, there is not one of them which can be a conclusion drawn from the other two. (Try it to check). In other words, you cannot use any two of the sentences to serve as reasons for the one that remains. All you have are three statements about computers. What about the next example?

> Children will be able to do their school work much better if they have access to a computer at home. The price of home computers has fallen considerably over the past few years. So parents should buy a computer for their children to use at home.

This is an argument. The conclusion ('So parents . . .') is supported by the reasons in the first two sentences. In other words there is an attempt to persuade parents to buy computers.

Questions
Now look at the passages which follow and work out which are arguments. (You'll need to show which parts are reasons and which conclusions.)

(1) Satellite television companies are increasingly bidding for the exclusive rights to televise live sport. Most people don't subscribe to satellite television. The technology of television is changing rapidly.

(2) Most people who visit zoos want to see lots of animals. Displays about endangered species, however well-presented, can never excite us in the same way as real lions and elephants. Zoos need to concentrate on providing lots of living animals rather than displays about them.

(3) Some zoos are trying to save endangered species in order to

return them to the wild. Wildlife programmes on television are very popular. Safari parks provide an opportunity for people to see animals wandering freely.

(4) Traffic-calming measures are increasingly necessary in residential areas. Cars are travelling much too fast along residential streets. Imposing speed limits has not slowed down the speed at which cars travel.

Answers

(1) This is not an argument. None of the sentences can serve as a conclusion drawn from the other two.

(2) This is an argument. The third sentence is the conclusion supported by the reasons in the other two. That zoos need to concentrate on providing animals rather than displays is justified by the claim that most people want to see animals and that displays about animals can never be as exciting as the real thing. This is the only way you can construct an argument with this passage, so if you got it any other way round, look at it again.

(3) This is not an argument. All you have are three statements about zoos, wildlife programmes, and safari parks. Whichever way round you put these, none of them would work as a conclusion drawn from the other two.

(4) This is an argument. The first sentence is a conclusion drawn from the other two. The reasoning works like this: since cars are travelling too fast along residential streets, and since speed limits have not worked, therefore traffic-calming measures are increasingly necessary. If you had this any other way round, look at your answer again.

RECOGNISING THE IMPORTANCE OF ARGUMENTS

Now that you can identify arguments, a question still hangs over the proceedings.

It's all very well learning what arguments are. But why do I need to know what they are?

This is a good question. After all, one of the claims that we are making in this book is that, if you can master the skills described here, you will be better able to handle the material you are studying.

Arguments are found everywhere. They are found in newspapers and magazines, on television and radio; they are found in every school and college subject, every debate, every court case. Some are good arguments, some are bad; some are so familiar that you wouldn't think of them as arguments; some will challenge many of your beliefs. It is partly because there are so many attempts to persuade us of one thing rather than another that we need to develop skills in assessing arguments. But it is also important for us to be able to develop our own arguments, especially if we are to become competent at dealing with arguments in academic subjects.

If, for example, you are studying the social sciences, you will meet arguments around every academic corner: arguments about the causes of crime, about social change, about the significance of the family, and so on. If you are studying history, you will also have to deal with arguments: these might include the significance of the French Revolution, the causes of the First World War, and the role of religion in social change.

Making judgements
Becoming competent at a subject is much more than knowing a series of facts. Obviously, not having the factual knowledge means that you're not going to get very far, but you also need to evaluate and analyse the material you're studying. Time and time again, you will be asked to carry out tasks which involve you making judgements about your material. From a requirement to do a specific analysis of information to the open-ended requirement to 'discuss' a general theme, you will benefit from having critical thinking skills.

ARGUING, EXPLAINING, AND SUMMARISING

Before we look further at arguments, we need to stop briefly to consider the difference between explaining, summarising, and arguing.

Explaining and arguing
Not everything that has the appearance of an argument is actually an argument. You will remember that in addition to reasons and conclusions, an argument should be intended to be persuasive. Look at the next example:

> The ship comes into port at 7.30. Passengers disembark 30 minutes later. Therefore the customs officers will be on duty by 7.55.

This example has the form of an argument, with what appear to be two reasons supporting a conclusion. But it is not a persuasive piece of writing: it is doing no more than explaining that will happen. It is not justifying one duty time rather than another for customs officers.

Thus we can distinguish between explanations and arguments in terms of the purpose for which they are produced.

This is not to say that explanations are of no interest in critical thinking. Very often, an argument will rely on a particular explanation to support its conclusion. In such cases, you will need to evaluate the explanation to see whether or not it does provide such support. Look at the following example:

> The forest fire was caused by some campers cooking on a barbecue and leaving the still-hot remains on the ground. If we are to reduce the risk of such a fire happening again, we must forbid camping in the forest.

In this example, the author is using an explanation for the forest fire in order to argue that we need to forbid camping. The explanation is not equivalent to the argument, but used as a reason for the conclusion. The explanation of the cause of the fire might be accepted, but someone might want to make the point that it is not enough to support the conclusion (for example, on the ground that one accident does not justify such a restriction).

Summarising and arguing

Another way of producing the form of an argument without having its persuasive purpose is in summarising. The next example will show how this works:

> Buying a house will involve spending time on looking at lots of very often unsuitable properties. It will also involve spending money on things like surveys. In addition, it will require plenty of patience and determination. So house-buyers will need to have time, money, patience, and determination.

As we have seen, the word 'so' often indicates the presence of a conclusion. But, in this case, the sentence beginning with this word is not a conclusion. The previous three sentences might also look like reasons for an argument, but the final sentence does not use them in this way. As you can see, the final sentence does no more with what comes before it than to summarise the content. It is not a conclusion based on reasoning. To highlight the difference, look at a version of the above in which the first three sentences are indeed used as reasons.

> Buying a house will involve spending time on looking at lots of very often unsuitable properties. It will also involve spending money on things like surveys. In addition, it will require plenty of patience and determination. Most people have little time, not much money, and very little patience or determination. So it is not worth their while trying to buy a house.

As you can see, the final sentence is not a summary of what comes before. It draws a conclusion based on the previous reasoning. In other words, it goes beyond what has been stated before. By its very nature, summarising can do no more than restate what has gone before.

MATCHING REASONS TO CONCLUSIONS

The distinction between summarising and arguing is a very important one to remember, in that it focuses our attention on the relationship between reasons and conclusions. We talk of a conclusion being drawn from the reasoning, so the reasons must provide sufficient support for the conclusion. If they don't, then it would be wrong to draw that conclusion.

This relationship between reasoning and conclusion can be illustrated by the following short exercise. Here you will find a conclusion followed by three options, only one of which could serve as a reason for that conclusion. Your task is to identify which of these three options could support the conclusion.

Exercise

Conclusion: Mobile phones should not be allowed on the company's premises.

Reasons:

(A) Most of the company's employees own a mobile phone.

(B) The use of mobile phones can interfere with the company's computers.

(C) Much of the company's business is done by fax rather than by phone.

Which of (A), (B) and (C) best serves as a reason for the conclusion?

Answer

The answer is (B). If mobile phones can interfere with computers, then this is a good reason for not allowing them on the premises, in that the company's business could be adversely affected.

(A) is not a good reason for the conclusion. Without other information, the claim that most employees have a mobile phone is not sufficient to conclude that such phones should be banned. (Other information could be that employees are spending too long on their mobile phones and thus not doing enough work.) You could combine (A) with (B) to give an even stronger argument than with (B) alone, but you can see that without something like the latter, (A) cannot be used as a reason for this conclusion.

(C) is also not a good reason. The significance of this might be that employees are not very likely ever to use mobile phones, but even this interpretation (and it's by no means an inevitable one) does not provide a sufficient reason for concluding that mobile phones should not be allowed.

Looking for relevance

When matching reasons to a conclusion, as in the above exercise, one of the things that you were looking for was **relevance**. You were asking yourself: is this evidence or statement relevant to such a conclusion?

There was some relevance in all of the possible reasons, but it was limited in (A) and even more so in (C). (A)'s relevance lay in its reference to mobile phones, and (C)'s in its reference to the company's use of phones. (B) was relevant not only in its reference to mobile phones, but also by its identification of a problem with such phones.

One thing that needs to be remembered when you are assessing reasons for relevance is that sometimes a reason on its own will be irrelevant, but with others its relevance will be clear. The mobile phones example has already illustrated this point, when we noted that (A), though irrelevant on its own, became relevant when put together with (B).

In assessing (A), (B) and (C) as reasons, you were looking for something in addition to relevance. You were also looking for **adequacy**.

Looking for adequacy

Though (A) and (C) has some relevance to the conclusion, neither was an adequate reason for it. Even if (A) or (C) are both true, neither is sufficient (alone or together) for the given conclusion. In other words, they do not provide sufficient support for the conclusion. (B), on the other hand, is enough on its own to support the conclusion. So how do we measure adequacy of a reason?

We look to see what the argument claims to do. If it seeks to prove something, then the reasoning must have a very high degree of adequacy. If, however, the conclusion us a fairly weak one, then the reasoning can be correspondingly weaker. To illustrate this question of adequacy, look at the next exercise.

Exercise
You are first of all given a set of different claims, followed by a series of possible conclusions.

Claims:
(A) The Government is 35 per cent behind in the opinion polls.

(B) The Government is not very popular.

(C) No political party has ever won an election from a position of the level of the Government's unpopularity.

Conclusions:
(1) The Government will lose the next election.

(2) The Government might lose the next election.

(3) The Government will probably lose the next election.

Work out which claims provide adequate reasons for which conclusions.

Answers
(A) would certainly provide an adequate reason to conclude (2) and

be acceptably adequate for (3). As you can see, (2) is a very weak conclusion, using only the word 'might', and so requires very low adequacy. (3), however, is more demanding by its use of 'probably'.

(B) would be adequate for no more than (2). Again, the undemanding nature of (2) is reflected in the less demanding reasoning required.

(C) would obviously be relevant for (2) and is slightly more adequate for (3) than was (A). This is because the evidence gives us more confidence in the conclusion, by giving us a stronger reason for the conclusion.

As you can see, no claim is sufficiently adequate for (1) in that this conclusion demands a very strong reason. It is, in fact, quite difficult to come up with a fully adequate reason for this conclusion. However, it is the sort of conclusion that is likely very often to be drawn. In reply, you would want to say that, at most, we are justified in drawing either (2) or (3), but, of course, you are beginning to be a critical thinker, so you would, wouldn't you?

Some people are not yet at this stage. It is time to meet them.

CASE STUDIES – INTRODUCTION

Three students will be used throughout the book to help us see how thinking critically can be viewed in different ways.

John, studying History: the uncritical student

John, aged 18, approaches his course material as something to be learned without having to make any judgements about it. It's an approach which reduces learning to listing what various authorities have said about a subject, even though these authorities might have significant disagreements about it. The idea of challenging the ideas is rejected on the grounds that 'I don't know enough about the subject'.

Hilary, doing Business Studies: the over-critical student

Hilary, a mature student, will not accept anything without having a discussion about it. This can have its virtues, but too often she does not expect the rules of argument to apply to her own evaluations. Statements like 'It's just common sense' or 'Nobody in their right mind would believe that' or 'You can do anything with statistics' pepper her responses. She is particularly intolerant of 'what if' arguments, in which an author looks at what might happen if you make certain (possibly unusual) assumptions.

Annie, doing Psychology: the critically thinking student

Annie, 21, looks at course material as something which should be evaluated, but recognises that such evaluation has to be carried out within a structure that is much more than simple agreement or disagreement. She is interested in how arguments are built up, at the sort of evidence which is relevant to them (and to evaluating them), and how she can usefully challenge (or confirm) what she is studying. Annie uses critical thinking to become a more creative student, not only usefully evaluating course material but also developing her own written work such that the ideas she uses have been well thought-out.

DISCUSSION POINTS

1. We have described arguments as being 'persuasive'. What would stop an argument being persuasive?

2. Write as strong an argument as you can against a position you would normally defend. Why are you not persuaded by this argument?

3. Write as strong an argument as you can for a position you would want to defend. How relevant and adequate are the reasons you have used?

2
Analysing Simple Arguments

IDENTIFYING REASONS AND CONCLUSIONS

Now that you can identify arguments by looking for reasons and conclusions, and you can make an initial assessment of reasoning, we
start by consolidating your skills in working out which part of an
argument is doing what.

When you come across arguments in books, newspapers and so
on, you won't usually find them neatly organised. Sometimes those
bits of a passage which make up the reasoning and the conclusion end
up obscured by irrelevance and illustration. Knowing which parts of
a passage are doing what will enable you to assess both the strengths
and weaknesses of the argument.

We start with a short exercise to test whether you can work out
which are reasons and which is the conclusion in a short argument.

Exercise
For each of the following arguments, identify which sentences are
reasons and which is the conclusion. They are labelled (A), (B) and
(C) to help in the discussion which follows.

(1) (A) For many victims of crime, a tougher prison regime for
criminals would be welcome. (B) The Government is right to
introduce tougher regimes in prisons. (C) Many offenders would
not commit crime if prisons had a tougher regime.

(2) (A) There should be no control over the right of newspapers to
publish photographs and stories about public figures. (B) The
lives of people who are public figures are of considerable interest to the general public. (C) People have a right to information
about how public figures conduct their lives.

(3) (A) The proposed anti-drugs campaign is unlikely to be effective

22

with young people who take drugs. (B) The proposed anti-drugs campaign will stress the risks involved in taking drugs. (C) One of the main attractions of drugs for young people is the excitement of taking risks.

Answers

(1) (A) and (C) are the reasons for the conclusion (B). The conclusion that the Government is right to introduce tougher regimes is supported by the two reasons that victims of crime would support such a change, and that fewer crimes would be committed. To see how (B) fits well as a conclusion, look at the rewritten version:

> For many victims of crime, a tougher prison regime for criminals would be welcome. Furthermore, many offenders would not commit crime if prisons were tougher. So the Government is right to introduce tougher regimes in prisons.

(2) (B) and (C) are the reasons for the conclusion (A). See how it reads when it is presented with (A) at the end:

> The lives of people who are public figures are of considerable interest to the general public. In addition, people have a right to information about how public figures conduct their lives. Therefore there should be no control over the right of newspapers to publish photographs and stories about public figures.

No other combination would work as an argument.

(3) (B) and (C) are the reasons for the conclusion (A). No other combination would work as an argument. To see how it works, look at it in a more organised version:

> One of the main attractions of drugs for young people is the excitement of taking risks. The proposed anti-drugs campaign will stress the risks involved in taking drugs. Therefore the proposed campaign is unlikely to be effective with young people who take drugs.

In this exercise, you were doing something very important. In working out which sentences were reasons and which conclusions, you were developing skills in structuring arguments. More specifically you were:

● looking at the relationship between reasons and a conclusion.

But what we must also do is to look at the **relationship between reasons** themselves. This can vary from argument to argument.

CHECKING ON THE WORK REASONS DO

But I already know what reasons do. They support a conclusion, if they're relevant and adequate. So what more checking do I need to do?

You're right, of course. You do know what reasons do, but what we haven't yet looked at is how reasons can do their work in different ways. Look again at the argument you worked on a short while ago:

> For many victims of crime, a tougher prison regime for crimi-nals would be welcome. Furthermore, many offenders would not commit crime if prisons were tougher. So the Government is right to introduce tougher regimes in prisons.

How do the two reasons support the conclusion? Do they do it in the same way as the reasons support the conclusion in the next example?

> Overcrowding in prisons is a cause of many prison riots, and most of our prisons are overcrowded. Thus riots in our prisons are likely in the coming months.

The answer is simple: no, they don't. In the first example, the rea-sons support the conclusion independently of each other. In other words, if you took either of them away, the other would still on its own enable the conclusion to be drawn. For example, let's take out the first reason.

> Many offenders would not commit crime if prisons were tougher. So the Government is right to introduce tougher regimes in prisons.

The conclusion is perhaps weakened by the loss of the point about victims wanting a tougher regime, but not to the extent that it cannot be drawn. Either reason in this example is both relevant and adequate.

In the second example, however, the reasons do not operate independently. If you remove either of them, the one that is left is insufficient for the conclusion. (Try doing it.) It is only by their acting together than we can draw the conclusion.

Why would arguments in which the reasoning does not operate independently be more vulnerable than those in which it does? Because each step in an argument in which the reasons operate together needs to be both relevant and adequate. For example, if you could show that most of our prisons were not overcrowded, then the conclusion about the likelihood of riots could not be drawn (even if the first reason was still true).

SHOWING ARGUMENT STRUCTURE AS A DIAGRAM

Though you do not have to use diagrams of arguments in order to be an effective critical thinker, it can often be useful in helping you to see quickly how an argument is structured. In turn, being able to see the structure quickly will help you in evaluating an argument. This applies not only to those that you'll meet in the various texts you'll use on your course, but also to those that you use in your written work. It's a useful check that the argument is working in the way you think it is.

We start with a very simple example. It's a shorter version of an argument that we met right at the beginning:

> Smoking's not illegal. Therefore people should be allowed to smoke anywhere.

In this argument, there's just one reason supporting the conclusion. To diagram its structure, we label the reasons as R, the conclusion as C, and the relationship between them by $\downarrow$

This gives us

$$R$$
$$\downarrow$$
$$C$$

If we look at the original version of this argument, we see that there were two reasons given for the conclusion:

People should be allowed to smoke anywhere. Smoking's not illegal, and millions of people get huge pleasure from it.

To show that there are two reasons, we give each reason a number:
R1: Smoking's not illegal.
R2: Millions of people get huge pleasure from it.
We can diagram this as follows:

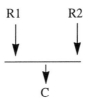

In this example, the reasons are supporting the conclusion independently so their relationship with the conclusion is shown accordingly. In another previous example, we had an argument in which the reasons acted together to support the conclusion:

(R1) Overcrowding in prisons is a cause of many prison riots, and (R2) most of our prisons are overcrowded. (C) Thus riots in our prisons are likely in the coming months.

How would we show this argument?

As you can see, this shows that the conclusion is drawn on the strength, not of each reason, but of the reasons acting together.

This technique of structuring an argument is much simpler than it might have seemed. The advantage of using it is to highlight what is doing what in an argument, with the result that you can assess its strength or weakness more easily. Before we move on, it will be useful to practise your skills in structuring arguments.

Exercise
Write out the structure of the following arguments. Label each reason accordingly (R1, R2, *etc*):

(1) Children are very susceptible to the power of advertisers. Those children who smoke tend to buy those brands that are most frequently advertised. It must be advertising that influences children to smoke.

(2) Divorce should be made easier rather than more difficult. Marital breakdown is distressing enough without separating couples having to worry about a difficult divorce. In addition, there is evidence that if the process of divorce is difficult, then a great deal more bitterness and anger is produced than if the process had been easier.

(3) Most people don't go to watch football matches. But the costs of policing them are very high. Clubs make a contribution to these costs, but most of the bill falls to us all to pay. Football fans must be prepared to pay higher prices for their tickets to cover most of these costs.

Answers
(1) This has a very simple structure.
R1: Children are very susceptible to the power of advertisers.
R2: Those children who smoke tend to buy those brands that are most frequently advertised.
C: It must be advertising that influences children to smoke.
R1 and R2 work together to support the conclusion (although it might be possible to draw the conclusion on the strength of R2 alone).

(2) In this argument, the conclusion appears first, followed by two reasons which support it independently.
R1: Marital breakdown is a difficult enough time without separating couples having to worry about a difficult divorce.
R2: There is evidence that if the process of divorce is difficult, then a great deal more bitterness and anger is produced than if the process had been easier.
C: Divorce should be made easier rather than more difficult.

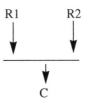

(3) This argument has three reasons which work together to support the conclusion.

R1: Most people don't go to watch football matches.

R2: But the costs of policing them are very high.

R3: Clubs make a contribution to these costs, but most of the bill falls to us all to pay.

C: Football fans must be prepared to pay higher prices for their tickets to cover most of these costs.

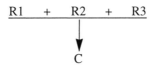

DISTINGUISHING REASONING FROM OTHER MATERIAL

In the examples we have looked at so far, the arguments have consisted of reasoning and a conclusion. You have not been asked to look for anything else. In the 'real world', however, arguments are not normally going to be presented so tidily. You might have to cut through all sorts of other material in order to get to the argument itself. Look at the next example:

> The showrooms of many garages are full of tempting offers to buy cars. These offers include interest-free credit, good part-exchange deals and many free extras. Manufacturers compete with each other to sell us fast, stylish dream-machines. But what about safety? There are already all sorts of safety features available, and a lot of evidence that motorists are not only less likely to have accidents if their car has these features, but also far more likely to survive any accident they're involved in. We should demand that car manufacturers concentrate on safety to the exclusion of all else.

In this example, the argument doesn't get going until half way through the passage. The first three sentences do no more than set the scene for the argument which concludes that we should demand that cars are made safer. The information on special offers provides something of a background for the argument but is not part of it.

Making appropriate responses

Why is it important to be able to distinguish between reasoning and other material?

The importance of being able to distinguish between reasoning and material such as illustrations and background information lies in your ability to make the appropriate responses to arguments. For example, faced with the passage about car safety, a response such as 'but many motorists are attracted by good part-exchange deals' would have missed the point. It is a response to an item in the background information rather than to the argument itself.

The following exercise asks you to distinguish an argument from any other material which accompanies it.

Exercise
Identify which part of each of the following passages is the argument:

(1) In the average dustbin you will find a wide variety of valuable resources: metal, paper, card and glass. Many of these items can be economically recycled. People should be encouraged to use local recycling facilities instead of throwing away things like paper, cans and bottles. Though manufacturers might give a great deal of thought to the packaging they use, too often they don't worry about what happens to it when it's finished with. Packaging which is attractive on the supermarket shelf is much less so when it is blowing across a pavement or littering our beaches.

(2) Many countries have a national lottery. The UK's National Lottery was introduced in 1994 and the level of participation in it has been much higher than the original estimates predicted. One of the worrying features of the National Lottery is that, following its introduction, the amount spent on gambling in the UK has gone up. The Lottery must have encouraged people to think of gambling as a solution to their financial problems. But people who have won large amounts by doing the football pools or the Lottery have not necessarily felt any happier as a result.

Answers

(1) The first three sentences provide the argument. It can be reduced as follows:

> Valuable resources are thrown away. Many of these could be economically recycled. Therefore people should be encouraged to use recycling facilities.

The remainder of the passage provides a criticism of manufacturers' use of packaging. Even though the final sentence seems to give a further reason for the conclusion, the argument is concerned with valuable resources being economically recycled. In consequence, the final sentence is linked to the recycling argument in only a very limited way (it could be just as easily linked to an argument on effective waste disposal).

(2) The argument consists of the third and fourth sentences. It is a fairly simple argument (but not necessarily a very good one): following the introduction of the National Lottery, the amount spent on gambling has gone up. Therefore the Lottery has encouraged people to think of gambling as a solution to their financial problems. The material which surrounds this argument is no more than background information (other countries and the date of the National Lottery's introduction) and a claim that winning money does not guarantee happiness.

DECIDING WHAT CONCLUSION CAN BE DRAWN

In most of the arguments that you'll be using or looking at, the most that you'll be able to conclude is that something is **probably** rather than **certainly** true. This is because there's always likely to be some claim or evidence that will not support the conclusion.

Concluding with certainty or probability

Arguments in which the conclusion can be drawn with certainty are called **deductive** arguments, whilst those which can be drawn with no more than probability are called **inductive** arguments. An example of a deductive argument is the following:

> If enough troops can be used for the peacekeeping force, then the civil war in Bosnia will be over. The United Nations has

promised that enough troops will be supplied, so the fighting in that country will end.

With this sort of argument, if the reasons are true, then the conclusion must also be true. In this example, if it is true that providing enough troops *will* end the civil war, then providing enough troops *must* end it. Look, however, at a different example of an argument on this subject:

The UN is planning to put troops into Bosnia. But, in the past, putting UN troops into countries which are fighting a civil war has not solved the problem. So this won't solve the problem.

In this second example, the conclusion (that putting troops into Bosnia won't stop the civil war) is drawn on the strength of previous experiences of putting UN troops into countries fighting a civil war. Though previous experience might well be a very useful guide to what will happen, it cannot be a certain guide, especially when it concerns the experience of different countries. You could think of all sorts of reasons why the conclusion could not be drawn. For example, the UN troops in Bosnia might be better equipped than were the previous UN troops, or the situation in Bosnia might have significant differences from other civil wars. In this sort of example, even if the reasoning is true, it does not mean that the conclusion must be.

As you can see, the conclusions of deductive arguments are true given the form of the argument itself. With our first example on UN troops in Bosnia, if you accepted the truth of the reasoning, then you had to accept the truth of the conclusion. In other words, it would have been illogical to agree with the reasoning but disagree with the conclusion. Any dispute you had with the argument would be with the reasoning.

Drawing different conclusions from the same reasoning

With inductive arguments, you can accept the reasoning but still question the conclusion. Thus people might come up with different conclusions from the same reasoning. For example, look again at the argument on gambling and the National Lottery which you met in the previous exercise.

Drawing one conclusion

One of the worrying features of the National Lottery is that, following its introduction, the amount spent on gambling in the UK has gone up. The Lottery must have encouraged people to think of gambling as a solution to their financial problems.

If you were given the claim that gambling in general has gone up since the introduction of the Lottery, can we conclude that the Lottery has caused the increase in gambling? It is a conclusion that people have indeed drawn, and in some ways it could be seen as a reasonable one (in that the introduction of the Lottery is certainly relevant evidence in considering why gambling has increased). But this conclusion does not have the status of certainty. You could draw a different conclusion from the same evidence.

Drawing a different conclusion

Following the introduction of the National Lottery, the amount spent on gambling in the UK has gone up. Therefore more people are addicted to gambling than before.

In this second example, the author sees the significance of the evidence in the same way as in the first, but goes further in the conclusion. It is a conclusion that requires the evidence to do quite a lot of work, in that it is quite a jump from the evidence. A third example, however, sees the significance of the evidence very differently.

Drawing another different conclusion

Following the introduction of the National Lottery, the amount spent on gambling in the UK has gone up. Therefore people who gambled before the Lottery are spending even more on it now.

In this example, the evidence is used to draw a conclusion about existing gambling rather than one about an increased number of gamblers.

In each example, the conclusion has no more than a probability of being true, such that we can accept the reasoning without accepting the conclusion. What you will have noticed is that the different conclusions are based on different explanations of the meaning of the evidence.

We will look at the general question of certainty and probability in more detail in Chapter 5. In the meantime you might have a more specific question.

Surely we can argue about some things with more certainty than we can about others. For example, arguments in science must be concerned with certainty rather than probability. Things are either true or they're not, aren't they?

Of course we can argue about some things with more certainty than we can about others. This would be where the facts of 'the case' are not in dispute. But whether or not we can conclude something with certainty still depends on the nature or form of the argument. Arguments in science – though they're dealing with 'facts' – are very often concerned with probability rather than certainty. This is because our knowledge is very often incomplete and we have to draw a conclusion on the strength of limited information. For example, it is a fact that some of the ice-caps in Antarctica are melting. But there is a big disagreement as to whether or not you can conclude from this evidence that therefore there is global warming. Look at the argument put in two different forms:

> If some of the ice-caps in the Antarctic are melting, this is evidence of global warming. Since they are melting, there must be global warming.

> Some of the ice-caps in the Antarctic are melting. Therefore there must be global warming.

In the first example, the form of the argument means that if the reasoning is true, then so must be the conclusion. In the second, the reasoning could be true, but the conclusion not be.

CASE STUDIES

John finds discussion too difficult

John has been given an assignment which asks him to discuss whether the French Revolution was the major turning point in modern history. He explains to his tutor that he's happy looking at the causes of the French Revolution and at describing the events at that time. But he isn't comfortable with the word 'discuss'. 'If a professor of history says it was the major turning point, then he must be certain that it is. What is there to discuss?'

Hilary finds there's not enough discussion

Hilary has been getting impatient with many of her tutors. 'They're not prepared to consider that they might be wrong. One of them gave us some figures on unemployment and argued that fairly high unemployment is likely to be a permanent feature in the UK. That seemed a bit vague, so I asked whether he could be sure. He just said the evidence seemed to point in that direction. But as I pointed out, unless you can be certain, you can't argue like that.'

Annie finds discussion clarifies her thoughts

Annie's group has been looking at the subject of intelligence testing, and there has been a lot of discussion as to whether it's of any value. Some of them are worried that we can't be certain that such testing actually measures intelligence. Annie points out that they should look to see how the supporters of intelligence tests argue their case. 'After all,' she says, 'unless we know what the argument is, we can't usefully criticise it.'

DISCUSSION POINTS

1. If one argument has far more reasoning than another, does this make the first argument much stronger than the second?

2. If you can't think of any reasoning which would challenge an argument, does this make the conclusion true?

3. If you can think of evidence which would challenge the reasoning of someone's argument, does this make your argument stronger than theirs?

3
Finding More Detail in Arguments

FINDING MORE THAN ONE CONCLUSION

So far we have looked at fairly simple arguments in which the author uses reasoning to draw a conclusion. But you are also likely to find arguments in which there is more than one conclusion drawn. What happens is that the author draws one conclusion and then goes on to use this in order to draw another one. Here is an example:

> Since some of the Antarctic ice-caps are melting, there must be global warming. So we can expect sea-levels to rise, resulting in catastrophic flooding of many of our coastal areas.

The conclusion of this argument is easy to spot ('So we can expect . . .'). But did you notice another conclusion that came just before it? Have a look again at the first sentence. It consists of an argument: some of the Antarctic ice-caps are melting, therefore there must be global warming. This conclusion is then used to draw the conclusion in the second sentence: there is global warming, so we can expect sea-levels to rise, resulting in catastrophic flooding of many of our coastal areas.

Using a conclusion as a reason

This example shows us what seems at first sight to be a strange thing: that a conclusion can be used as a reason. The conclusion about the rise in sea-levels was drawn from the claim that there is global warming. If we extend the argument even further, you can see that the conclusion about rising sea-levels can itself be used as a reason for a further conclusion:

> Since some of the Antarctic ice-caps are melting, there must be global warming. So we can expect sea-levels to rise, resulting

in catastrophic flooding of many of our coastal areas. We should take action now to reduce the causes of global warming.

In order to clarify which conclusion is which, we make a distinction between a main conclusion and an intermediate one.

- The **main conclusion** is the one towards which the whole argument is heading; an **intermediate conclusion** is one drawn on the way.

- An argument can have an unlimited number of intermediate conclusions, but obviously only one main conclusion.

How would we put these intermediate conclusions into our method for diagramming the structure of arguments?

We can use our first example to show this:

(R) Since some of the Antarctic ice-caps are melting, (IC) there must be global warming. (C) So we can expect sea-levels to rise, resulting in catastrophic flooding of many of our coastal areas.

Look at the next example. Can you find an intermediate conclusion in it?

The pollution in our rivers is increasing at a fast rate. The more polluted a river is, the more damage is done to the animals that live in it. Unless we soon do something about river pollution, the numbers of many water creatures in our rivers will decline. However, there are no effective plans to reduce the amount of river pollution. Therefore, many of the creatures that live in our rivers will not survive.

The third sentence is the intermediate conclusion, with the first two serving as reasons for it. If you are unsure of this, read the first three sentences again, ignoring the final two. This intermediate conclusion, together with the fourth sentence, is then used to draw the main conclusion. Look again at how this works:

> Unless we soon do something about river pollution, the numbers of many water creatures in our rivers will decline. However, there are no effective plans to reduce that amount of river pollution. Therefore, many of the creatures that live in our rivers will not survive.

Fitting intermediate conclusions into the structure

As you can see, the intermediate conclusion acts as a reason supporting the main conclusion. We would diagram it in the following way:

> (R1) The pollution in our rivers is increasing at a fast rate. (R2) The more polluted a river is, the more damage is done to the animals that live in it. (IC) Unless we soon do something about river pollution, the numbers of many water creatures in our rivers will decline. (R3) However, there are no effective plans to reduce the amount of river pollution. (C) Therefore, many of the creatures that live in our rivers will disappear.

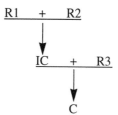

The importance of recognising intermediate conclusions lies in being able to see how an author builds up an argument. If you are able to show that an intermediate conclusion could not be drawn (or that a different one could be), then you have made a significant evaluation of that argument. In addition, if you can show that the intermediate conclusion could be drawn, but that how it is used as a reason for a further conclusion is dubious, you will be able to see which part of an argument is working and which isn't. In the same way, you will be able to keep a good check on your own reasoning. In order to practise your skill in finding intermediate conclusions, do the next exercise.

Exercise
In each of the following arguments, you will find an intermediate conclusion. Identify it and show how it fits with the rest of the reasoning.

(1) The plan for the new by-pass should be rejected. It's not supported by the majority of the local people, and it would spoil many notable beauty spots. A recently developed alternative scheme is, however, very popular with local people. The Government should reopen the public enquiry on the bypass.

(2) The Government has told the Prison Service to reduce its expenditure. However, the number of people being imprisoned is increasing. Prison staff will find it increasingly difficult to cope with the increased numbers. The Government could make savings elsewhere. Clearly, it should not reduce its expenditure on prisons.

(3) There are laws against the ill-treatment of farm and domestic animals. The reasoning behind these laws is that animals should not be allowed to suffer needlessly. But there are no differences in their capacity to suffer between wild animals on the one hand and pets and farm animals on the other. We cannot justify treating wild animals differently from any others. It follows that we should have a law against ill-treating wild animals.

Answers
(1) The intermediate conclusion is the first sentence. It's drawn from the content of the second sentence:
(R1) The plan for the new by-pass isn't supported by the majority of local people. (R2) It would spoil many notable beauty spots. (IC) Therefore it should be rejected.
This intermediate conclusion is then used together with a further reason to support the main conclusion:
(IC) The plan should be rejected. (R3) A recently developed alternative scheme is very popular with local people. (C) Therefore the Government should reopen the public enquiry.

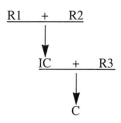

(2) The intermediate conclusion is the third sentence, and is supported by the reasoning in the first two. The reduction in expenditure and the increase in numbers lead to the conclusion that staff will find it difficult to cope:

(R1) The Government has told the Prison Service to reduce its expenditure. (R2) However, the number of people being imprisoned is increasing. (IC) Prison staff will find it increasingly difficult to cope with the increased numbers.

This intermediate conclusion is then used with the claim that the Government could make savings elsewhere (R3) to draw the main conclusion (C) that the Government should not reduce its expenditure on prisons. As you can see, the structure is identical to that in the previous argument.

(3) The intermediate conclusion is the fourth sentence. It is supported by the reasoning in the first three (note how the argument is built up step by step):

(R1) There are laws against the ill-treatment of farm and domestic animals. (R2) The reasoning behind these laws is that animals should not be allowed to suffer needlessly. (R3) But there are no differences in their capacity to suffer between wild animals on the one hand and pets and farm animals on the other. (IC) Therefore we cannot justify treating wild animals differently from any others.

This intermediate conclusion that we cannot justify treating wild animals differently is then used as the reason for the main conclusion:

We cannot justify treating wild animals differently from any others. (C) Therefore (in that we have a law protecting farm and domestic animals) we should have a law against ill-treating wild animals.

In this example, we have an intermediate conclusion being used as a reason on its own to support the main conclusion:

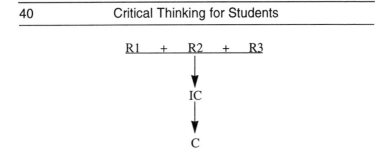

FILLING IN THE GAPS IN REASONING

So far we have been looking at arguments in terms of reasoning which is explicitly presented. In other words, we have been concerned only with those parts of the argument which are stated. However, many arguments will have other parts which, though not stated, play as important a role as those parts which are. We call these unstated parts **assumptions**.

You will have heard the word 'assume' being used to dismiss someone's argument. 'You're just assuming that' is an accusation that 'you have no proof of that'. This is not really the way in which we are using the term here. An assumption is an unstated part of an argument *without which* the conclusion could not be drawn. This usage can be made clear by looking at an example.

Looking for assumptions

> Most of the children at the school performed less well in GCSEs and A-Levels than children at other schools in the area. The quality of the teaching must be to blame.

In this example, the conclusion that it is the quality of the teaching which is to blame for poor examination results is based on only one reason. But in reality it has to be based on more than the reason which is stated. To conclude that the poor results are the result of poor teaching assumes that there aren't other explanations for the results. For example, it must be assuming that there are no relevant differences between the children in the different schools. It has to assume this because, if it didn't, the conclusion could not be drawn (without showing why this assumption was irrelevant). You will probably be able to think of other assumptions being made in this argument.

Clarifying the effect of an assumption
Here is another argument:

> If people had invested their money in antiques 20 years ago,
> they would have found it difficult to make a profit on their
> investment until very recently. So people who cannot afford for
> their savings not to increase should invest their money in
> something other than antiques.

What assumption is being made here? In that there is only one
reason and one conclusion, you can see that any assumption being
made must be a further reason operating between the two. The
missing reason required for the conclusion to be drawn is that 'the
price of antiques over the past 20 years is a useful guide to their
price in the future'. Without this assumption, the conclusion could
not be drawn. To see this more clearly, try putting the opposite of
this assumption ('. . . is not a useful guide') into the argument. The
effect is the same as turning the explicitly stated reason (the first
sentence) into its opposite: the conclusion would simply not
follow.

Thus, when you are producing or evaluating arguments, you
need to look at the assumptions which are being made in the same
way that you look at the reasoning that the author makes explicit.

Exercise
Identify any assumptions required in each of the following
arguments.

(1) Marco Polo is best known as the first person from the West to
have visited China. But in his writings about his visit there, he
nowhere mentions the Great Wall, tea or porcelain. Therefore he
can't ever have visited China. His book about his travels to that
country must have been written using information he'd picked
up from those people who had been there.

(2) In schools where special 'enrichment' classes are given to gifted
children, we find that such children do particularly well at all of
their subjects. Society needs highly intelligent and talented
people. Thus we need to ensure that enrichment classes are
provided in all our schools.

(3) All animals being brought into Britain are subject to a period of quarantine to ensure that they are not carrying rabies. This system of preventing rabies from entering the country has worked very well for many years, such that we have no cases of the disease. Any proposals to end these regulations must be vigorously opposed.

(4) For 20 years, children have been treated to all sorts of programmes on television which are supposed to help them become better at skills such as reading and maths. These programmes have presented the learning of skills such as counting and recognition of letters as nothing but fun, to be accompanied by such things as rainbows and jumping frogs. But no improvement in children's abilities in literacy and numeracy has been observed. These fun ways of teaching such skills obviously don't work.

(5) Boxing is the only sport whose main purpose is to render the opponent unconscious. Indeed it is the only sport in which each player is licensed to injure the other. It must then be the most dangerous of all sports. Various solutions to this problem have been proposed – such as the use of head-guards and changing the gloves – but none of these would solve the problem of the danger of serious injury. So boxing should be banned.

Answers

(1) The structure of the argument is as follows:

R1: Marco Polo is best known as the first person from the West to have visited China.

R2: But in his writings abut his visit there, he nowhere mentions the Great Wall, tea or porcelain.

IC: Therefore he can't ever have visited China.

C: His book about his travels to that country must have been written using information he'd picked up from those people who had been there.

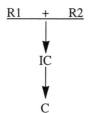

A: This is needed between R2 and IC. The assumption required is that 'travellers to China would have seen the Great Wall, tea and porcelain.' If this assumption is not made, we cannot use the reasoning about his failure to mention these things to draw the conclusions that he did not visit China.

(2) The structure of the argument is as follows:

R1:   In schools where special 'enrichment' classes are given to gifted children, we find that such children do particularly well at all of their subjects.

R2:   Society needs highly intelligent and talented people.

C: Thus we need to ensure that enrichment classes are provided in all our schools.

A: You might have found two assumptions. The conclusion that we need special classes for gifted children in every school assumes that every school will have gifted children. A further assumption required for this conclusion is that such special classes are the only way to ensure that we have 'highly intelligent and talented people'. It could be that other methods – for example, using different teaching materials in normal classes – would also help gifted children to realise their potential.

(3) The structure of the argument is as follows:

R1: All animals being brought into Britain are subject to a period of quarantine to ensure that they are not carrying rabies.

R2: This system of preventing rabies from entering the country has worked very well for many years, such that we have no cases of the disease.

C: Any proposals to end these regulations must be vigorously opposed.

A: An assumption is necessary for the author to be able to draw the conclusion. This is that 'no other system of rabies control can work'. Unless this assumption is made, the author cannot move from the claims about the present system to a recommendation that no other system can be supported.

(4) The structure of the argument is as follows:

R1: For 20 years, children have been treated to all sorts of programmes on television which are supposed to help them become better at skills such as reading and maths.

R2: These programmes have presented the learning of skills such as counting and recognition of letters as nothing but fun, to be accompanied by such things as rainbows and jumping frogs.

R3: But no improvement in children's abilities in literacy and numeracy has been observed.

C: These fun ways of teaching such skills obviously don't work.

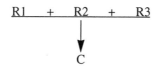

$$R1 \quad + \quad R2 \quad + \quad R3$$

$$\downarrow$$

$$C$$

A: You will probably have found at least one assumption in this argument. Perhaps the most obvious is that which must be slotted in between R3 and the conclusion. This is that 'the absence of any evidence of improvement is sufficient evidence of the ineffectiveness of the fun methods'. Without this assumption, the move from the reasoning to the conclusion cannot be made, in that the evidence might be interpreted in other ways. For example, we might say that the evidence shows that we need to have even more of such fun programmes in order to get the level of children's skills to rise.

Another assumption which you might have identified fits between R2 and R3. In order to claim R3, the author has to assume that any improvements in children's skills will be found using existing tests of such skills. If the fun method had changed the way children approach reading and maths, then the existing tests might not be able to identify this change.

(5)   The structure of the argument is as follows:

R1:   Boxing is the only sport whose main purpose is to render the opponent unconscious.

R2:   It is the only sport in which each player is licensed to injure the other.

IC: It must then be the most dangerous of all sports.

R3:   Various solutions to this problem have been proposed – such as the use of head-guards and changing the gloves – but none of these would solve the problem of the danger of serious injury.

C: So boxing should be banned.

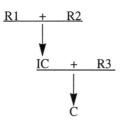

A: The move from R1 and R2 to the intermediate conclusion
     might seem to be one which does not require an assump-
     tion. It is such a familiar way of thinking that we might not
     question the move, especially as the media are often report-
     ing on the dangers of boxing. But if you stop and think
     again, you should be able to see that an assumption *is* being
     made here. This is that the *purpose* of boxing – the deliber-
     ate infliction of injury, and rendering the opponent uncon-
     scious – in itself makes the sport 'the most dangerous of all
     sports'. In other words, the purpose of boxing is the same
     as the practice. Boxing might be a very dangerous sport, but
     we cannot conclude that it is the *most* dangerous from evi-
     dence of its purpose without making this assumption. Other
     sports might be more dangerous even though their purpose
     is not to cause injury. (Examples might be rugby, horse
     riding, skiing and mountain climbing.)

     This example of an assumption serves to show us that argu-
     ments might not be as strong as their authors believe. This
     one contained a very questionable assumption, one which,
     when removed, weakens the argument.

USING ANALOGIES

We sometimes find an argument (or use one ourselves) in which part
of the reasoning is based on the assumption that one situation is sufficiently similar to another to enable a conclusion to be drawn on the
strength of this similarity. An example will clarify this:

     So-called 'experts' on children often urge parents to allow their
     children to have as much freedom as possible in exploring their
     'environment'. They argue that children are naturally curious
     about the world and so should not be prevented from finding

out all about it even if this is sometimes inconvenient to their parents. But think what it would be like if animals – who are also naturally curious – were given the freedom to explore their 'environment' without any control. There would be chaos. Therefore we should pay little attention to the views of these experts.

In this example, the author argues against 'experts' on children on the grounds that, if their views on children were applied to animals, 'there would be chaos'. But the author assumes that the example of animals is sufficiently similar to that of children to show that the experts' argument should be rejected. The author does not argue why the two cases of children and animals should be seen as being sufficiently similar for this conclusion to be drawn: the similarity is assumed both in the sense that it is not argued for and in that this must form part of the reasoning.

Looking for similarities and differences

In assessing an analogy used in an argument (whether it is our own or someone else's) we need to look at it in terms of the similarities and differences between the two things being compared. If the similarities are much stronger than the differences, then the analogy is a good one; if the differences dominate, then it is a weak one. A strong analogy lends good support to the conclusion; a weak one lends little, if any, support. But it needs to be stressed that, however good the analogy, it can never make the conclusion beyond doubt. Before you move on, consider how effective is the children/animals analogy used in the first example.

Here is another argument containing an analogy:

> There has been a huge growth in the number of alcoholic drinks – such as alcoholic lemonade – which are designed to look as if they are no more than 'fun' drinks. These drinks are marketed as drinks for young people, in a campaign which stresses the fun more than the alcohol. The sales and marketing of these drinks must be much more rigidly controlled than they are now. We wouldn't tolerate a campaign by tobacco companies which targeted the young with chocolate-flavoured cigarettes.

In this example, the conclusion that the 'fun' drinks sales and marketing must be controlled more than they are at present is drawn from only one reason. This is that we wouldn't tolerate what is taken to be similar action by tobacco companies. Of course, the word 'similar' is the crucial one here. An analogy is being drawn between 'fun' drinks such as alcoholic lemonade (which are already on sale) and chocolate-flavoured cigarettes (which are not). As you can see, the argument depends upon the strength of this analogy: if it is not a good one, neither is the argument.

Checking analogies for relevance and adequacy
When we're assessing the reasoning of an argument, we're supposed to look at the relevance and the adequacy of the reasoning. Do we do the same thing when we're assessing analogies?

Yes, we do. In assessing any analogy we look for relevance and adequacy in the same way that we look for these qualities in any other type of reasoning.

If we take relevance first, in what ways is the analogy in this example relevant? It uses a situation in which we would condemn a 'fun' version of a product which we would want to discourage the young from using. It uses a situation in which the 'real' product is being disguised.

In what way is it adequate? The problem with it is that its strength is meant to come from its appeal to consistency: if you don't accept one situation, then you shouldn't accept another which is similar to it. But the chocolate-flavoured cigarettes don't exist: the appeal to consistency depends on an imaginary example. In other words, the adequacy of the analogy is weaker than a real example would have provided. However, the analogy highlights something. It makes us question the idea of these 'fun' drinks by showing us a scenario which, though imaginary, contains the essence of the problem. This, then, is its strength.

When someone uses an analogy in an argument, they must assume that the two situations are sufficiently similar either to draw the conclusion on the strength of it or to use it, along with other reasoning, in support of the conclusion. It will be your task, both in evaluating other people's arguments and in producing your own, to assess analogies in terms of the degree of similarity between the two situations.

CASE STUDIES
John resists making assumptions
John was asked to produce a seminar paper on why Hitler invaded Poland in 1939. He read to his group an account of what happened,

describing in some detail some of the military tactics used by the German army. He was surprised to hear his tutor, in expressing disappointment with the paper, make the specific point that its purpose was to try and understand the assumptions that Hitler made about the probable response of countries such as Britain. He needed to argue why, not to describe how. John was puzzled. As he said to her, 'Surely the point of history is to describe what happened. There's no argument about that: Hitler did invade Poland. All these questions about why he did don't get us very far.'

Hilary asks for facts

One of Hilary's lecturers has been looking at different styles of management. He made the point that each style is based upon different assumptions about human behaviour. Hilary was impatient with this explanation. 'How can human behaviour be assumed to be one thing or another? Human behaviour is what it is; it's not something we can just start making assumptions about it, like whether or not there's life on Mars.' Her lecturer tried to explain that human behaviour is not as simply dealt with as that, but Hilary retorted that 'managers should deal in facts, not academic arguments about how people behave'.

Annie dismantles an argument

Annie's group has been looking at the debate over the biological and social explanations for gender differences. Instead of dismissing one side or the other in terms of the conclusions they come to, Annie has been looking at the assumptions that have to be made for these conclusions to be drawn. For example, one piece of research used rats and altered the hormonal levels of both males and females. Whilst some of her fellow students either accepted or rejected the conclusions of the study, Annie pointed out that the conclusions were based on a number of assumptions about the relevance of research on rats to human gender differences.

DISCUSSION POINTS

1. The longer an argument is, the more assumptions are likely to be made by the arguer. Does this mean that longer arguments are potentially weaker than short ones?

2. Some arguments use analogies which are vague. Why might that be a source of both strength and weakness in their ability to persuade?

4
Exploring Weaknesses

What do you think of the following argument?

> All the great thinkers have had one thing in common. Look at pictures of Plato, Galileo, Marx, Darwin and Freud. What do you notice? They've all got beards. So their greatness must somehow be attributable to this fact.

It's pretty obvious, isn't it, that there's something wrong with it – but what, exactly? Quite simply, even though it has the structure of an argument, the conclusion doesn't follow from the reasoning ('all the great thinkers had beards, therefore their beards caused their greatness'). Even if all the great thinkers have had beards, we would not see this quality as the cause of their greatness, unless there was some evidence showing how such a causal link was possible. This example of a rather obviously poor argument starts us off on an examination of some of the ways in which arguments can show weaknesses. In this chapter we'll look at some of these weaknesses so that you'll be able both to spot them in others and avoid them yourself. We start by making a distinction between what are called **necessary** and **sufficient** conditions.

BEING NECESSARY AND BEING SUFFICIENT

Look again at the example on great thinkers. Even if it could be shown that their beards were somehow a contributory cause of their being able to think in profound and significant ways, it does not follow that having a beard is a guarantee of greatness. In other words, even if it could be shown that having a beard was something you had to have to be great thinker – a *necessary* condition for greatness – it does not follow that having a beard is enough for greatness – a *sufficient* condition.

This somewhat frivolous example of a bad argument has illustrated a very important point. Let's look at the different relationships involving necessary and sufficient conditions in more detail.

X might have no association with Y
If X and Y are found together, this association could be nothing more than coincidence, X being neither a necessary nor a sufficient condition for Y. You could think of many examples of this type of association. With regard to the bearded great thinkers argument, if we could find an instance of Y (great thinker) without X (beard) – either the beardless Isaac Newton or Einstein would be enough – this would destroy it utterly.

X is a necessary condition of Y
In these cases, when X is not present, Y cannot occur. We assume that beards are not a necessary condition for great thinkers, otherwise, if there is no beard, there is no great thinker. An example of a necessary condition is 'if you want to run the full distance of the London Marathon, you have to be fairly fit'. In this example 'being fairly fit' is the necessary condition: nobody could run the full distance of the London Marathon without meeting this condition. In the shorthand form used earlier, when X (being fairly fit) is not present, Y (running the full distance) cannot occur.

As you can see, being fairly fit is certainly a necessary condition for running the full distance of the Marathon, but it is not a sufficient condition. In other words, it is not enough for being able to run the full distance: you could be fairly fit but still not be able to complete the length of the course.

X is a sufficient condition for Y
In other words, where X is present, Y **must** occur. The author of the great thinkers argument, it will be remembered, believed that having a beard was a sufficient condition for greatness of thought. This was, of course, incorrect. So what could be an example of something being a sufficient condition?

The heir to the throne is the eldest son of the reigning monarch.

As you can see, being the eldest son of the reigning monarch is enough to make you heir to the throne: no other quality is needed. You don't have to be of a certain age, educational level, marital status or whatever: being the eldest son is a sufficient condition. In practice, however, there will be some exceptions – the most obvious being when the reigning monarch has no children or only daughters – and thus one could say that being the eldest son is a sufficient but not a necessary condition.

Distinguishing easily between necessary and sufficient conditions

The difference between necessary and sufficient conditions can be summarised very simply:

> If a necessary condition for X is absent, then X won't occur (or will be false); if a sufficient condition for X is present, then X must occur (or be true).

You will have seen that necessary and sufficient conditions apply both to causes and definitions. Our example of who meets the conditions required to be heir to the throne is one of definition; the example of beards and great thinkers was one which showed muddled thinking on conditions and causes.

Exercise
For each of the following, work out the relationship between X and Y. This relationship will be one of the following:

● a necessary condition

● a sufficient condition

● neither a necessary nor a sufficient condition

● both a necessary and a sufficient condition.

(1) X: smoking cigarettes; Y: developing lung cancer

(2) X: driving above the legal blood-alcohol limit; Y: being convicted of driving above the legal blood-alcohol limit

(3) X: having three A-Levels; Y: getting a place on a degree course at university

(4) X: the Labour Party winning a large majority of seats in the House of Commons; Y: the Labour Party forming a Government

(5) X: having all six numbers in the National Lottery draw on a valid ticket; Y: being at least one of the winners of the jackpot prize.

Necessary and sufficient conditions exercise: Answers

(1) In that there are examples both of people who smoke cigarettes but who don't develop lung cancer, and of people who develop lung cancer who don't smoke cigarettes, X is neither a necessary nor a sufficient condition for Y.

(2) In that some people drive above the legal limit without being caught by the police, X is not a sufficient condition for Y. But in that one cannot be convicted of driving above the limit without having driven in this condition, X is a necessary condition for Y. (Of course, we have to assume that the legal system convicts only those who are guilty of an offence, an assumption which we shouldn't really make. As a result, you would also be right if you'd used this reasoning to produce the answer that X is neither a necessary nor a sufficient condition for Y.)

(3) Unfortunately, having three A-Levels does not guarantee a place on a degree course, so X is not a sufficient condition for Y. Furthermore, degree course staff offer places to people with two A-Levels (and with one or with no A-Levels at all), so X is not a necessary condition for Y.

(4) If the Labour Party were to win a large majority of the seats in the House of Commons, then it would be called upon by the monarch to form a Government. No other realistic outcome would follow (we can discount a coalition between parties other than Labour, because of the effect of the word 'large'), and so in this example X is a sufficient condition for Y. However, it is not a necessary condition in that the Labour Party could form a Government without a large majority and without a majority at all (if it was still the largest party in the House of Commons or as part of a coalition).

(5) If you have a valid ticket with all six numbers, then you are

guaranteed to be at least one of the winners of the jackpot prize. Without such a ticket, you will not be one of the winners (however much you might dream). In this way, then, having such a ticket is both a necessary and a sufficient condition for being a jackpot winner.

CONFUSING CAUSES AND CONSEQUENCES

Some arguments put together evidence or claims in such a way as to conclude that one thing causes (or some things cause) another. Here is an example:

> The summer last year was the hottest on record. This year travel agents are reporting very poor sales of foreign holidays. Therefore people are assuming that this year will be as hot as last year and will be booking holidays in this country.

This argument uses two pieces of evidence (the hot summer and the poor sales) and concludes that there is a causal connection between the two, such that the poor sales are a consequence of the hot summer. It is an example of what is sometimes referred to as a *post hoc* argument, from a Latin phrase which in full means 'after this, therefore because of this'. In this example, it is assumed that since the fall in bookings followed the hot summer, the hot summer is the cause of the fall in bookings.

Looking for different explanations

When you meet this sort of argument (or indeed when you use it), you need to consider whether or not this cause/consequence relationship can be supported. Your main concern is whether or not there could be a different explanation for the consequence. In our example, how else could we explain the poor sales of foreign holidays? Of course, there could be no connection at all between the two pieces of evidence. The poor sales of foreign holidays could be explained in terms of economic uncertainty (the level of holiday bookings reflects the level of people's confidence in their financial state so many months hence) or in terms of dissatisfaction with foreign holidays, or in other ways. On the other hand, the hot summer could be one of many factors which could explain the poor level of bookings. As a result, one could not conclude that people have decided to holiday in this country only because of the hot summer.

Looking for different assumptions

There is another aspect of the argument which needs to be considered. The conclusion is drawn on the assumption that people are planning to take holidays (even if they're not booking foreign holidays through travel agents). If you take this assumption out, then the conclusion simply doesn't follow. Are there any other assumptions that are being made? The author must assume that the present level of bookings is a good guide to people's intentions (people could have various reasons for postponing making a decision). This example shows again how important an examination of the assumptions of an argument can be.

Look at another example and apply your critical skills to it:

> Cigarette advertising on television was banned 30 years ago. Since then we have seen the level of smoking fall. If we banned all cigarette advertising, then the level would fall even more.

How would you respond to this argument? Is the conclusion justified by the evidence? Is this merely a *post hoc* argument? Think of other possible explanations for the consequence that the level of smoking has fallen. What assumptions does the author need to make for the conclusion to be drawn?

Assessing the strength of causal arguments

Though arguments which use a causal explanation are not always justified, sometimes they might be very strong. Look at the following pair of arguments. Which is the stronger?

> Over the past few years, we have seen an increase in the number of cars which are fitted with 'bull bars'. Over the same period there has been an increase in the number of fatal road accidents involving pedestrians. Clearly the fitting of 'bull bars' should be banned.

> The fitting of 'bull bars' to the front of cars should be banned. Accidents involving pedestrians and those cars which have them fitted show a much higher rate of fatal injuries than in accidents involving cars without them. It is the rigidity of the bars which is responsible for the fatal injuries.

Looking at the evidence critically

In the first argument the conclusion is drawn from two items of evidence: the increase in the number of cars with 'bull bars' and the increase in the number of fatal accidents involving pedestrians. The conclusion that 'bull bars' should be banned is drawn on the assumption that the second piece of evidence is a consequence of the first. The weakness of the argument, of course, lies in its having failed to explain why there is a causal relationship between the two.

In the second example, two pieces of evidence are again put together to support the conclusion that the fitting of 'bull bars' should be banned. The first is that fatal accidents involving cars with 'bull bars' and pedestrians are at a higher rate than those involving cars without them. An explanation of this higher rate is given ('the rigidity of the bars') and the same conclusion drawn. But this argument is much stronger than the first. Unlike in the first, there is an attempt to show why there is a causal explanation. Furthermore, the two items of evidence do have a common link: the rate of fatal accidents in two situations in which the difference might well be highly relevant (and whose relevance is given emphasis by the explanation).

Asking questions about the evidence
As you can see, then, you should creatively evaluate arguments in which relationships between pieces of evidence are used to draw conclusions.

● Consider whether the evidence is sufficient to draw the conclusion.

● Are there other explanations as plausible as the one needed for the conclusion to be drawn?

● Ask yourself whether there needs to be any relationship between the evidence, such that if one accepts one piece one must accept (or reject) another.

● What assumptions must the author be making? Evaluate these assumptions.

● How could the argument be made stronger (as in the second of the pair above)?

Apply this same questioning rigour to your own work.

ATTACKING THE ARGUER RATHER THAN THE ARGUMENT

In this type of argument, an opposing argument is dismissed not by any reasoning which exposes weaknesses in it but by an attack on those who make it. Here is an example:

> Some people advocate that prisoners should be treated more harshly. They say that prisons should have none of the comforts of modern life, such as television and radio. If there were such harsh conditions, they argue, then fewer people would commit crimes. But these are just the sort of people who think nothing of avoiding paying income tax or of driving their car after an expenses-paid alcoholic lunch. We should therefore ensure that prisons are not places of harsh punishment.

In this argument, the conclusion is based on no more than the contents of the fourth sentence. Those who argue for greater harshness in prisons are attacked and this attack is used to reject their argument. As you can see, their argument is not, however, touched: the author gives us no (relevant) reasons why we should conclude that we must ensure that prisons are not places of harsh punishment. Even if it is true that proponents of harsh conditions are happy to avoid paying income tax or are drink-drivers, these qualities cannot be used to dismiss their argument that harsh prison conditions would reduce crime.

You will sometimes see this type of argument referred to as an *ad hominem* argument, the Latin phrase meaning 'against the man'. Though such personal attacks are very often irrelevant in an argument, there might be occasions when they are relevant.

Relevant attacks upon the arguer

> The managing director insisted that the company would not be making any compulsory redundancies this year, but she has made other similar promises in the past and has never kept them. Given that she has a long history of not being truthful with the workforce, her assurances about redundancies should not be believed.

In this argument, the conclusion that the managing director's assurances should not be believed is based on the reason that she has lied about the subject before. This attack on her sincerity is relevant in this argument in that it gives a good reason for the conclusion. In the following argument, however, it doesn't:

> The managing director insisted that the company could not increase its pay offer since profits were expected to fall substantially over the coming year. But she has been convicted of drink-driving twice in the past three years, so the union should not believe her profits forecast. They should press ahead with the strike.

In this second example, the managing director's sincerity is dismissed on a pretty obviously irrelevant ground. This attacks the arguer without attacking the argument, in that there is no good reason given for not believing her profits forecast. (You'll find this type of obviously irrelevant reasoning in some tabloid newspapers. It's a frequently-used method of discrediting someone with whom the paper disagrees.)

GOING ROUND IN CIRCLES

Some arguments might seem as if they've gone somewhere, but in reality they've gone nowhere. These are the arguments that conclude no more than the reasoning they use. An example will clarify this:

> Differences between the roles that males and females are expected to play are not fixed by our genetic make-up but are learned in each individual's social development. Thus gender is something that is learned rather than something which has a biological cause.

In this argument the author starts with the claim that gender roles are not biological in origin ('not fixed by our genetic make-up'), but are learned in social development. The conclusion does no more than repeat the claim. The argument has not moved from a reason to a conclusion: it has ended where it started.

Although in some cultures mere repetition of a point strengthens an argument, these circular arguments should not persuade us to accept the conclusion in that there is no reasoning which enables us to draw the conclusion.

Checking for reasoning

Sometimes an argument might look suspiciously circular, but closer examination reveals that some reasoning has been provided:

> The history of human society is full of examples of males being the hunters. Therefore there must be some truth in the biological explanation of males being hunters.

In this example the conclusion about males being the hunters is drawn from evidence on males as hunters; though there is a similarity in the words used, you can see that there is a shift in the argument from reason to conclusion.

RUSHING DOWN SLIPPERY SLOPES

The problem with circular arguments is that they don't go anywhere; the problem with slippery slope arguments is that they go too far too quickly. An example will show you the problem:

> The present proposal to allow ramblers greater access over private land needs to be resisted. If we were to allow this measure – small though it might seem – then we would end up having to allow far more extensive measures. What is to stop the principle of ramblers' rights of access being applied to small pieces of land such as a small orchard? Then, if you allow free access to such small pieces of land, the next step is access to people's gardens whether large or small. And there is a very small step from free access to people's land – however small the plot – to similarly free access to their homes. The whole idea of private property, indeed of privacy itself, will be threatened.

In this argument the author concludes that the proposal to allow greater access over private land to ramblers should be resisted. The reasoning for this conclusion goes down a slippery slope from having to allow access to small pieces of land such as orchards to a threat to private property (and privacy) via having to allow access to gardens and homes. As you can see, the reasoning takes us a very long way from allowing ramblers access to land. The weakness of the argument is that any of the steps taken down the slippery slope can be challenged and, if they are challenged, then what follows is unconvincing.

The slippery slope is a set of interconnected reasons, each of which is necessary for the whole structure. As a result, if we could show that the author of the above argument could not even make the first step in the reasoning – the shift to 'small pieces of land' – then what follows cannot be used to support the conclusion. The problem with slippery slope arguments therefore lies in their taking too many too big steps.

BUILDING STRAW MEN

In order to attack an opponent's arguments, we sometimes present it in a way that more effectively fits our critical purpose. We highlight what we take to be its weakest elements and then exploit these weaknesses. Sometimes our own arguments are presented and attacked in this way. This is all to do with persuasiveness, the basis of argument. But when arguments are *distorted* in order to exploit weakness we have what is often referred to as a 'straw man' argument. The significance of the term is that instead of dealing with the real argument (with all its substance and strength), we are dealing with a flimsy version of it (with none of the original's substance and strength). The distorted version is then attacked *as if* the real version had been. Here is an example.

Weaving a straw man

> The urban cyclist is increasingly intolerant of other forms of urban transport. In their campaign to get more cycle lanes in our cities they use every opportunity to attack the private motorist. They see the car as the cause of a vast range of respiratory diseases, and of a host of other urban problems, including crime. But they ignore all the positive contributions which the private car has made to modern life. It has given people freedom: to go out with their family, to visit friends and relatives, and to make things such as shopping much easier. Until the cycle lobby is prepared to approach the subject of urban transport in a more reasonable way, it should not be listened to.

The straw man in this argument is fairly easy to spot. The urban cycle lobby is described as having a campaign to get more cycle lanes in cities. If we accept that this is true, then we would expect to find some sort of argument against an increase in cycle lanes, giving the conclusion ('the cycle lobby . . . should not be listened to'). But there is no such argument. All we find is an attack upon a position ascribed to the cycle lobby: 'They see the car as the cause . . . they ignore all the positive contributions. . . '. This position is described as unreasonable (an unreasonableness which is easy to defend), but the reasonableness (or otherwise) of the cycle lane issue is not considered. In this way the cycle lobby is attacked by means of a straw man.

You might think that the straw man type of argument is very similar to the attacking the arguer rather than the argument method. There is a similarity in that the real argument is not dealt with, but the method is different.

TURNING TWO WRONGS INTO ONE RIGHT

We are all familiar with this line of argument in that it's one which children tend to use:

> It's not fair that I got into trouble for forgetting my books. Lots of kids in my class forget their books.

In this argument, the reasoning for the conclusion that 'it's not fair . . . ' is that 'lots of kids' do the same thing. As you can see, though this argument appeals to a simple form of justice, it is unconvincing. It is alarming, however, how often it is used by those who should know better:

> The Leader of the Opposition can hardly accuse us of distorting the truth. He wasn't telling the truth when he said that he would support all measures to combat crime.

In this all too familiar type of argument, an accusation of not being truthful is not actually dealt with. Instead, a counter-accusation is made. As critical thinkers we are not persuaded by this argument in that, even if the Leader of the Opposition hadn't been telling the truth, this does not enable the arguer to conclude that they should not be accused of lying.

You can see why this type of argument is sometimes referred to as a 'you too' argument (or by the Latin phrase *tu quoque* which means the same thing). They are not good arguments in that the reasoning is neither relevant nor adequate. Watch out for them: be harsh with those that others use and avoid using them yourself.

Appealing to consistency

However, sometimes you will find arguments that look as if they are 'you too' arguments but which seem to have some strength to them. Have a look at the next example:

> The industrialised world frequently complains to those countries which have the world's rain forests about the need to stop cutting down these forests. The world's climate, they say, will be severely damaged if the destruction of the rain forests continues. The protection of the world's environment is, they argue, the most important problem now facing humanity. But the countries with the rain forests reply that the industrialised world is much more guilty than they are of using up scarce resources and of damaging the environment. So the rich industrial countries should stop going on about the destruction of the rain forests and look at their own behaviour.

Checking for relevance

In this argument you will have spotted the counter-accusation in the fourth sentence. It has an obvious 'you too' quality to it. But is the counter-accusation irrelevant? In the politician example, the irrelevance of the counter-accusation lay in its complete failure to deal with the accusation of lying. Quite simply, *even if* the Leader of the Opposition has told lies in the past, this point does not answer the accusation. However, in the argument about the rain forests the counter-accusation has some relevance. If the central point of the complaint by the industrialised countries is a concern for the environment, then evidence that they are being inconsistent in their approach to environmental issues is relevant. In other words, the 'you too' accusation is a relevant response to the initial accusation, identifying a sniff of hypocrisy.

This example showed us that there is room in argument for an appeal to consistency. In the rain forest example, the argument against the industrialised countries is that, given their position – the protection of the world's environment is the most important problem now facing humanity – their right to complain about the destruction of the rain forests has to be considered. (In the above example about whether the Leader of the Opposition can accuse the Government of lying, the argument would have had some merit if it had been one about consistency. In other words, if the Leader of the Opposition had taken up a position in which no politician should ever lie, and had been known to lie.)

RESTRICTING OPTIONS

You will remember that the problem with the 'straw man' argument was that the opponent's position was presented in a deliberately weak way in order to argue against it easily. There is another way in which a possible counter-argument is presented in such a way that it looks weaker than it might really be. Look at the next example:

> The problem of the vast numbers of pigeons in our towns and cities can be approached in one of two ways. We can either ignore the problem, allowing the numbers to continue to increase with all the consequences of disease and damage to buildings which will follow. Or we can embark on a wide-spread campaign of shooting and poisoning of the birds in order to make very significant reductions in their numbers. Since this second option will deal with the problem of disease and damage, it is the one which we should adopt.

The author offers no more than two solutions to the problem of urban pigeons and, given the way in which the options are described, only one of them is supported. As a result, the problem of the pigeons would be solved, according to this argument, by 'a widespread campaign of shooting and poisoning'.

However, the author has played an argumentative trick on us. They have led us to the conclusion by ignoring any other options available. It could be that these other options would not lead us to support the recommended campaign. For example, there could be the option of putting down food laced with a contraceptive in order to keep the numbers down. Another option would be to seek to reduce the incidence of disease by putting down food laced with anti-parasitic medicine. You can probably think of others.

Notice how the author's second option is apparently given strength by the weakness of the first. In other words, the first option is presented in such a way that the author has already taken you by the hand to look for a different one.

MAKING IRRELEVANT APPEALS

There are many examples of arguments in which the arguer seeks to strengthen their argument by making an appeal to something that's irrelevant. We'll look at two of these types of appeal and show why they do not work.

Appealing to popularity

Some arguments are based, at least in part, upon reasoning which appeals to popularity. Here is a simple example:

> Most people believe in one or more superstitions such as bad luck following a walk under a ladder or if a single magpie is seen. So there must be some truth in superstitions.

In this argument, the conclusion that there must be some truth in superstitions is based only on the evidence that most people believe in them. There is no further reasoning. But we need much more evidence than most people's belief in superstitions before we can conclude that 'there is some truth' in them. In this sort of example, truth is a matter of evidence of a causal link between the superstition and events which follow it. Even if everybody believed in such causal links, the truth is still a matter of evidence of them.

But are there not some types of argument in which an appeal to popularity is relevant?

Yes there are. In the previous example an appeal to popularity was irrelevant in that people's belief, however widespread, was not relevant to the conclusion. This is because truth in a case such as this is established by evidence not by belief. But there are arguments in which widespread support for something is relevant to drawing a conclusion. An obvious example is the following argument:

> Most people support the Bill to ban hare coursing. So MPs should vote in support of the Bill.

In this argument, the appeal to popularity is relevant in that whatever the case for or against hare coursing, if most people favour a ban on it, MPs have to at least consider the strength of public feeling. This argument is not about the truth of whether or not hare coursing is cruel (defined in terms of pain and suffering of the hare) but about whether or not MPs should vote to ban it. Political and social judgements in a democracy need to consider the evidence of popularity.

Appealing to pity

In some arguments the conclusion is drawn by appealing to pity. Here is an example:

The national poetry competition was recently won by Lady Fiona Grant, the heir to the Grant millions. This is unfair. There are plenty of poets who entered the competition who really needed the £5,000 first prize. Lady Grant didn't need the money at all.

In this argument, the conclusion that Lady Grant's winning the competition was unfair is based upon the reasoning that she didn't need the money whilst other poets did. But this reasoning is irrelevant if the criterion of winning the competition was poetic ability.

Making pity a relevant appeal
Appeals to pity fail if they are irrelevant; however, you might be able to think of arguments in which they would be relevant. These would be arguments in which there is no criterion which overrides the appeal to pity (unlike in the previous example where, though other poets might well have needed the money more than did Lady Fiona, their need – and her lack of it – were irrelevant). Here is an example in which an appeal to pity is relevant:

> The National Poetry Fund has recently received a bequest from Lady Fiona Grant's estate to provide grants for young poets to enable them to develop their work. The Fund has narrowed their choice of who should receive the first grant down to two people: George Hamilton and Lucy Chapman. Both have shown considerable promise in their work but Hamilton has to work long hours in a factory in order to live whilst Chapman does no more than a bit of part-time teaching. It's obvious that the grant should go to George Hamilton.

This argument uses an appeal to pity (in the form of an appeal to need as the primary consideration) to draw its conclusion. Why is this appeal relevant? Because, unlike in the first example, the criteria used to decide on who should get what include that of need. Again, then, we are evaluating arguments according to relevance.

There are many other examples of arguments based on irrelevant appeals. Use your critical skills to assess them when you meet them.

Exercise
Identify the weakness in each of the following arguments:

(1) Those who argue that the rain forests should be protected from

further development are the sort of people who don't want to see progress. Progress has brought us all sorts of benefits, such as medical care and rapid transportation. People's lives would be much poorer if our predecessors had stood in the way of progress. We should not therefore listen to those who oppose the proper development of the rain forests.

(2) Over the past few years we have seen a huge growth in the number of students in higher education. This growth must result in a disturbing dilution of standards, with too many students being awarded degrees. As the standards of degrees fall, so too will the confidence which employers place in their worth. With more and more graduates being unable to find work, we will find that the universities will be unable to recruit very talented young people who will decide to develop their talents in more productive ways. Thus the present policy of encouraging large numbers of people into higher education will have the effect of failing to develop the abilities of the highly talented few. It should be abandoned as soon as possible.

(3) Increasing the price of cigarettes will reduce the number of people who smoke. The price has been going up over many years and the level of smoking has been declining.

(4) Michael MacGregor, the Secretary of State for Social Security, has announced that he will not be approving an above-inflation increase in the basic pension. He argues that the country simply cannot afford to pay more than a three per cent increase. But all this argument about us not being able to afford to pay a decent pension for our old people is so much nonsense. MacGregor's elderly parents are nicely set up in their ancestral castle, without a financial worry to trouble their wrinkled brows. It's clear that the MacGregor family has no idea what poverty our old people are suffering. We should therefore keep pressing for an increase in the pension to a level way above three per cent.

(5) Research on what are called 'health farms' has shown that people who have attended then feel much healthier as a result. All of the health farms in the study had regimes which included special diets and massage. We can conclude therefore that, if

people want to feel healthier, they should follow a special diet and have a programme of massage.

(6) The current policy on prisons is to make the regimes increasingly tough for inmates. The problem is that once you've produced these tough regimes, and you see that they don't reduce the level of crime, you're faced with the problem of having to make them much more liberal. Discipline in prisons will be so inconsistent that chaos will follow. We should try to stop this move towards tougher prisons before it is too late.

Answers

(1) This describes the position of those who oppose the development of the rain forests in terms which have a 'straw man' look to them. The description of them as not wanting 'to see progress' enables the arguer to attack them by referring to various benefits of progress. In that standing in the way of progress is seen as a bad thing, so too is (therefore) opposition to the development of the rain forests. It is not difficult to see that this 'straw man' description of the position of those who oppose the development of rain forests is a distortion of their position, a distortion which enables the arguer to ignore any strength in their real position.

(2) This has a familiar 'slippery slope' look to it. The shift from increased student numbers to a decline in standards is made without any reasoning to show why there must be such a decline. Similarly, the shift from graduates being unable to find work to talented young people not wanting to go to university is a big step without sufficient reasoning.

(3) This is a *post hoc* argument. The author puts together two items of evidence and assumes that there is a causal relationship between the two. The increase in the price of cigarettes might have caused the decline in the number of smokers, but the decline could be explained in other ways, unrelated to the changes in price (for example, the health education campaign).

(4) You will have spotted the *ad hominem* argument here. Whether or not the elderly parents of Michael MacGregor are living in luxury does not affect his argument that he will not approve an

above-inflation increase because the country can't afford more. His argument needs to be addressed in terms such as showing that we could afford more (by savings elsewhere, for example) or that we should increase taxes to pay for the increase. Attacking MacGregor on the grounds that he doesn't understand the problem of poverty amongst the elderly is partly relevant to an argument about whether or not old people need more money, but it is not relevant to his argument about the economics of the problem.

(5) This is another *post hoc* argument. Though the evidence is consistent with low-fat diets and massage being the cause of people 'feeling healthier', we cannot say that they are that cause. There are many things which we can say about this evidence. For one thing, it could be that either diets or massage was responsible for the 'feeling healthier', not the two together. It could be that 'health farms' also have other features which were the true cause (for example, a fitness centre). It could be that just being away, being rested and pampered, is enough to make people feel healthier. As it stands, this argument suffers from the weakness that the evidence does not unequivocally support the conclusion (even though it is relevant, it is not adequate).

(6) This is an example of restricting the options. The author presents no more than one option following the predicted failure of the tougher prison regimes. This is that we would have to replace the tougher regimes with those which are 'much more liberal'. Following this one option, chaos is further predicted. But there need not be just one option. Even if the tougher regimes didn't reduce the level of crime, they could be justified in other ways, or the option is there to make them tougher still (or one could make them just a little less tough). A further option could be to combine the tougher regimes with other crime-reduction measures. Thus the conclusion that we should try to stop the move towards tougher prisons is based upon a distortion of the options available.

CASE STUDIES

John, Hilary and Annie assess hypothetical arguments

John's group has been discussing a number of those familiar hypothetical arguments which arise in history: for example, would the history of Europe have been different if people like Napoleon, Hitler, Luther and so on hadn't been born? But John finds such arguments very weak. 'All of these people were born and did do what they did, so any sort of argument which looks at what would have happened if things had been different must be pretty pointless.'

Hilary is similarly unhappy with spending time on hypothetical arguments. 'My tutor has been playing what he calls "imaginative games" with us. It's all stuff like "if a company prices its goods higher than those of its competitors, then in some situations the demand for its goods will go down but in others might go up. So, if a company lowers its prices, the same thing will happen." Then we're meant to come up with explanations for this. The problem with those sort of exercises is that they don't get anywhere. "If this" and "if that" don't add up to proper arguments.'

Annie's group has been considering the problem of whether perception is something that is learned or whether it is inborn. The problem has been presented to them in the form of a number of hypotheticals. One of them is that if perception has to be learned, then the quality of the learning experience must affect the way in which an individual perceives things. Annie finds such hypothetical arguments very useful. 'They show you what you have to look for in order to make a good argument. For example, with this one, it shows us that we have to look for evidence of the effect of different learning experiences.'

DISCUSSION POINTS

1. Why do some arguments seem to be persuasive even though they're based on one of the weaknesses in reasoning we've just been considering?

2. When might it be appropriate to attack someone's personal qualities even though they're putting forward a perfectly good argument?

3. What would be wrong with an argument which was based on the reasoning that since something has not been proved to be false, it must be true? Can you think of an example of this type of reasoning?

4. What would be wrong with an argument in which the conclusion was based on the reasoning that since something has not been shown to be true, it must be false? Can you think of an example of this sort of argument?

5
Finding Strengths

LOOKING FOR CERTAINTY

In Chapter 2 we briefly considered the distinction between **deductive** and **inductive** arguments. You will remember that the first type provided arguments in which, if the reasoning was true, the conclusions must also be. In inductive arguments, on the other hand, even if the reasoning is true, the conclusion will only be at best probably true. In virtually all of the arguments we have looked at so far, the conclusion – even if it was supported by both relevant and adequate reasoning – was never more than probably true.

Making the conclusion follow

We now look at a few further examples of arguments in which their form rather than their content gives them their strength (although the first will remind you of a type of argument which we met when looking at weaknesses in reasoning). There we considered the problem of arguments in which options are restricted. Now look at an example of an argument in which if the restriction of options is not a distortion of the truth, the conclusion must follow:

> With such a small majority, the Prime Minister must either abandon the Government's legislative programme or try to attract support for it from members of other parties. He is determined to press ahead with the programme, so he must start to attract support for it from the other parties.

In this example, if the two options *are* the only true options available, then the conclusion *must* follow: it is not probably true but certainly true. Thus, when evaluating arguments, you need to consider arguments in which alternatives are presented. If the alternatives exhaust the possibilities, then the conclusion must follow. But if you can show that the author has failed to consider at least one other possibility, then the conclusion does not follow with certainty (and indeed might well be a case of an argument with restricted options).

Considering alternatives

This highlights an important part of how you will use your critical thinking skills. When dealing with an argument whose reasoning depends on a restricted number of options, you need to consider whether the options presented (or which you present) are exhaustive. If they are, then the conclusion can be drawn with certainty. If they are not, any conclusion drawn (including any you draw) can have only a degree of probability.

Looking at the form of an argument

The truth of its reasoning is central to the strength of an argument. In a deductive argument, one could not have true reasons supporting a conclusion which is false. Similarly, in an inductive argument, truth links the reasons with the conclusion in that their truth increases the probability that the conclusion is true.

But as well as looking at the content of an argument we should also look at its form or structure. This will often tell us a lot about the argument's strength or weakness. The example above highlighted to us that, if the options were exhaustive, then the form of the argument required that we accept the conclusion. This alerts us to the potentially persuasive quality of deductive arguments. We can now look at some other forms. One of these builds up a chain of reasoning.

Building a chain of argument

In this form of argument, each reason links with the others. Here is an example:

> If the Government doesn't implement the recommendations of last year's report on the transport of oil by oil tankers, then another accident at sea will happen soon. Were such an accident to happen, then the marine and costal environment will be further damaged. Therefore, if the Government doesn't implement the report's recommendations, we can expect further environmental damage.

In this example, two parts of the reasoning are linked together into a hypothetical conclusion. As you can see, the entire argument is a series of hypothetical statements ('if . . .') in which a chain is built

up: if A is true, then B is true; if B is true, then C is true; therefore if
A is true, then C is true (check this shorthand against the argument to
see how it works). In this type of reasoning, if the initial links in the
chain are true, then the conclusion can be drawn with certainty.

In assessing (and using) this type of argument, you need to look at
whether the links in the chain are properly equivalent. In other words,
given its structure, you have to be sure that those parts which are
meant to be the same really are. Look at the next example:

> If the Government doesn't implement the recommendations of
> last year's report on the transport of oil by oil tankers, then
> another accident at sea will happen soon. Were such an acci-
> dent to happen, then the marine and coastal environment will
> be further damaged. Therefore, if the Government doesn't have
> an answer to its critics, we can expect further serious environ-
> mental damage.

In this second version of the oil pollution argument, there is no
equivalence between 'doesn't implement the recommendations . . .
oil tankers' and 'doesn't have an answer to its critics'. The argument
is not a chain in that there is no longer a continuous series of links
between the components of the argument. There has been a sleight of
hand shift in the argument, in which the conclusion might at first
glance seem to be OK. But with your critical evaluation skills, you
can quickly see the problem.

Denying what comes after

Another type of argument in which the form provides its strength is
one which is often referred to as 'denying the consequent'. You need-
n't worry about using the proper term, but being able to recognise (and
use) this form will be useful. An example will show you how it works:

> If the penguin population is not to be seriously threatened, then
> we have to stop the oil companies from drilling near the
> penguins' breeding grounds. But the campaign to stop the oil
> companies has failed, so there is now a significant threat to the
> penguin population.

In this example, the form of the argument provides its strength. If
you translate it into the terms we used earlier, you get 'if A is true,
then B is true; B is not true, therefore A is not true'.

Denying what comes before

You will need to be on your guard for arguments which look as if they might have a structure which gives them strength, but whose structure is crucially different from those which do. Look at the next argument for an example of this:

> If the new theory of the explanation of life on Earth had been accepted, our understanding of the nature of evolution would have needed to be substantially revised. But the new theory has not been accepted, so our understanding of evolution does not need to be revised.

This argument might have the appearance of strength. It looks as if it has a good tidy structure whose conclusion follows with certainty. But it has a crucial weakness. Quite simply, the conclusion does not follow. Even if the new theory has not been accepted, we might still have to revise our understanding of evolution in the light of other explanations. In other words, the rejection of this one theory does not enable us to conclude that we do not need to revise our understanding of evolution. To emphasise the difference between this argument and one in the previous form, look at another version of it:

> If the new theory of the explanation of life on Earth had been accepted, our understanding of the nature of evolution would have needed to be substantially revised. Since our understanding of evolution does not need to be changed, the new theory cannot have been accepted.

In this version, the conclusion must follow: if an acceptance of the new theory *requires* a revision in our understanding of evolution, then if our understanding does not need to change, the theory can't have been accepted.

INCREASING PROBABILITY

In the previous section we looked at how the structure of an argument can sometimes enable us to conclude with certainty. Of course, the proviso was, as always, that the reasoning must be true. We now look at how we can strengthen arguments in which we draw conclusions not with certainty but with some degree of probability.

You will remember that we use the tests of relevance and adequacy in determining whether an argument's reasoning can support the conclusion. In the same way, we can use these tests to strengthen an argument. This can be done in one of two ways:

● by extending the range of the reasoning

● by limiting the range of the conclusion.

We will look at each of these.

Extending the range of the reasoning

In seeking to strengthen an argument, we can add to the reasoning some further evidence which is relevant to the conclusion. As you can see, by doing so, we are increasing the degree of adequacy of the reasoning. Look at the next example:

> Our courts are open to the public because 'justice should be seen to be done'. But most people have never been to a court, especially one in which a case is being heard. Clearly, therefore, the proceedings of courts should be televised.

This argument has two reasons supporting the conclusion. As you will have noticed, the reasons operate together. How would you extend the reasoning in order to strengthen the argument? You will probably be able to think of ways of doing this. Examples include the following:

● 'there is considerable public support for the televising of court proceedings'

● 'many lawyers and judges are in favour'

● 'evidence from the US where court proceedings are televised shows that there is considerable public interest in them'

● 'there is evidence that criminals are inhibited from committing crime by the prospect of being shown on national television'.

Each of these items of further reasoning would strengthen the argument by providing more support for the conclusion. Each is relevant to the conclusion and each increases the degree of adequacy of the reasoning. If you added all of them into the argument, it would be considerably strengthened.

Limiting the range of the conclusion

The conclusion of the above argument was that court proceedings should be televised. This is a general recommendation. What happens if we reduce the range of this conclusion, by making it less general?

> Our courts are open to the public because 'justice should be seen to be done'. But most people have never been to a court, especially one in which a case is being heard. Clearly, therefore, we should try an experimental scheme in which the proceedings of some courts are televised.

The conclusion is narrowed in two ways. Instead of a general recommendation that court proceedings should be televised, there is one for an experimental scheme only. This less general recommendation strengthens the argument by cutting off some of the possible lines of counter-argument. In particular, it deals with the objection that there might be all sorts of problems with televising court proceedings. The second way in which the less general conclusion strengthens the argument is in its specification of 'some courts' rather than simply 'courts'.

Again, this specification cuts off the counter-argument that it might not be appropriate for some cases to be given such widespread public coverage.

As you can see, limiting the range of the conclusion has the effect of making the conclusion less demanding of its reasoning. It allows the reasoning to be less comprehensive, to be (as you would now recognise) less adequate.

To **strengthen** any arguments that you use you should, therefore, do at least one of the following:

● provide further relevant evidence

● limit the force of your conclusion.

So to **weaken** any arguments that you come across (and to identify any weakness in your own) you will need to do at least one of the following:

● produce evidence that supports an opposing conclusion

●   identify any irrelevance in the author's reasoning

●   identify any inadequacy in the author's reasoning.

Exercise
In this exercise you are given a short argument. Using the evidence which follows it, which items of evidence would strengthen the argument, which would weaken it, and which would have no effect upon it?

Argument: The number of prisoners who take illegal drugs whilst in the prison has shown a very large increase over the last year. A system of searching every visitor to the prison must be introduced.

Evidence:
1.   The number of prisoners in the prison has increased substantially over the past year.

2.   Some visitors to the prison have been found to be carrying illegal drugs.

3.   Most prisoners in the prison take illegal drugs.

4.   Most prisoners in the prison used illegal drugs before they were admitted to prison.

5.   A drug education programme has just been started in the prison.

Answers
Let's look first at the argument. It's pretty obvious what's going on. The author is assuming that the increase in the number of prisoners taking illegal drugs is explained by the drugs being brought in by visitors. Without this assumption (as further reasoning), the conclusion cannot be drawn. Thus to strengthen the argument we must use evidence which strengthens this line of reasoning (in that no other line is used).

By providing an alternative explanation for the increase in drug-taking, (1) has the effect of weakening the conclusion. In other words, if we can explain the increase in the number of prisoners taking illegal drugs simply in terms of an increase in the number of prisoners (the proportion not having changed), then the recommendation of a new system of searching visitors is not easily supported.

(2), on the other hand, strengthens the argument. Given that the author has assumed that the increase in drugs is explained by visitors bringing them into the prison, any evidence that supports this line of reasoning will strengthen the argument. Slot it into the argument and see how it does this.

(3) has no effect on the argument, unless it is tied to the assumption that visitors are bringing the drugs in. But unlike (2) which provides evidence to support the conclusion, (3) does little more than fill out some of the detail of the first sentence.

(4) has no effect on the argument. Even if most prisoners did take illegal drugs prior to their imprisonment, this evidence cannot be used to support a system of searching visitors. Furthermore, even if we accept this evidence as true, it is not incompatible with the claim that most prisoners in the prison do not take illegal drugs.

(5) would weaken the argument. In that it offers a different strategy for dealing with the drugs problem (a strategy that is moreover already in place), the conclusion ceases to have the same force.

CASE STUDIES

John is overwhelmed by facts
John is finding it difficult to use facts in order to evaluate arguments. 'There are so many facts that we have to learn, but when it comes to using them in an essay I seem to be just listing them rather than using them. I'm not clear about how I should go about working out which to put in and which not.'

Hilary wants no more than facts
Hilary's patience has run out. 'All this evaluation gets us nowhere. It's pretty obvious to me whether an argument's good or bad. It's good if the facts are right and it's bad if they're not. All we need is a list of which facts are right and then we can cut through all this evaluation business. That's the trouble with all these lecturers. They think everyone can sit around worrying about this and that. Like I told them, out in the real world thing's aren't like that. Decisions have to be made or companies would go under.'

Annie finds a way through the facts
Annie finds that thinking carefully about the arguments she wants to

present helps her sort out not only which facts to look for but also which she needs to use. 'When you've got really big subjects to look at – like intelligence and behaviour – you can get overwhelmed by all the evidence around. But just thinking through the arguments you've got to look at helps you to start working out what's relevant and what isn't. It's really a more efficient way of working.'

DISCUSSION POINTS

1. If you can find evidence of one case which doesn't support an author's conclusion, does this mean that their argument fails?

2. If you can find a large number of cases which support your argument, does this mean that your argument is certainly true?

3. Hilary thinks that worrying about arguments has no relevance to the real world. 'Decisions have to be made or companies would go under.' How would you show her that making decisions and using arguments can be very similar?

How to Write Your Dissertation
A practical survival guide for students
Derek Swetnam

Almost all advanced educational courses now include a dissertation or research project of some type. For many students this can be a terrifying experience as the time for submission approaches and tutors are elusive. This book offers a plain guide to ways of producing an excellent dissertation with minimum stress and frustration. It covers choosing a subject, planning the total work, selecting research methods and techniques, written style and presentation. The author is a former Course Leader of a large Master's level programme at the Manchester Metropolitan University.

£8.99, 102 pp illus. paperback. 1 85703 164 4.

Available from How To Books Ltd, Plymbridge House,
Estover Road, Plymouth PL6 7PZ.
Customer Services tel: (01752) 202301. Fax: (01752) 202331.

Please add postage & packing (£1 UK, £2 Europe, £3 world airmail).

Credit card orders may be faxed or phoned.

6
Applying Your Skills

There was a book available in the 1920s which taught children to swim without them ever having to get into water. It did this by showing them all the strokes that were needed for both arms and legs, strokes that they were asked to practise whilst lying on the bedroom carpet. The assumption which is crucial to this teaching technique is that the skills learned on the bedroom floor are able to be transferred to the rather different reality of the swimming pool. There is little point in being able to execute a perfect breast-stroke on the bedroom carpet if all is forgotten in two metres of water.

In the same way, this book will not have achieved its purpose if, having worked through it, you cannot apply in your own work the skills it has tried to give you. In other words, when you have to write an essay or report, when you have to give a presentation, when you have to assess information for whatever purpose, you should do it using your critical thinking skills.

ASKING THE RIGHT QUESTIONS

When you are assessing a passage which contains at least some argument, you need to ask the right evaluative questions. But before you can do this, you need to work out what the argument is:

- What conclusion does the author come to?

- What reasoning does the author use to support this conclusion?

- What assumptions are necessary for this conclusion to be drawn?

These are the basic questions which you need to ask before you can begin to evaluate the argument. Unless you can see what the argument is, you can't assess its strengths and weaknesses. Having found the argument, now ask questions to evaluate it:

● Does the reasoning support the conclusion?

This is a general question, one which you will always have to be asking. In practice, this general question will become a series of specific questions:

● Does the evidence have the significance that the author intends?

● Are there explanations for the evidence which would change its significance for the argument?

● If the author uses any analogies, do they work?

● What happens if different assumptions are made?

● What sort of evidence would strengthen the argument?

● What sort of evidence would weaken the argument?

● Does the reasoning support a different conclusion?

Try this questioning technique with the following short arguments. Though they have the same newspaper-type heading, they are very different arguments. Read version 1 first and think about its strengths and weaknesses before you read version 2.

Version 1: Some smokers have tried to get compensation from the tobacco companies on the ground that smoking has damaged their health.

> Given that smoking is addictive and that the tobacco companies knew that it was, they should have done something to reduce the addictive nature of cigarettes. Instead, they controlled the level of nicotine in cigarettes in order to keep smokers hooked. Not only that, since the publication of the report by the Royal College of Physicians in 1962 it has been known that there are serious dangers with smoking. Manufacturers of any product have a legal duty to minimise risks to their customers. In that tobacco has been known to be both addictive and harmful, the tobacco companies should compensate smokers who have become ill as a result of smoking.

Version 2: Some smokers have tried to get compensation from the tobacco companies on the ground that smoking has damaged their health.

The tobacco companies have responded by arguing that people who smoke choose to smoke. Nobody is forced either to start or, having started, to continue. Furthermore, half of all smokers manage to give up smoking. In addition, given that it has been known for many years that smoking is harmful – since the Royal College of Physicians report in 1962 – smokers should have given up smoking. All the tobacco companies were doing was responding to a demand from smokers. If smokers can get compensation from tobacco companies, what comes next? Law suits against drinks manufacturers over cirrhosis of the liver? An action against the dairy industry by heart-disease sufferers? Clearly, people who smoke should not be given any compensation.

Looking at the significance of evidence

As you can see, these two arguments come to completely opposite conclusions. But, in doing so, they used some reasoning which was common to both. This is the 1962 report of the Royal College of Physicians which highlighted the dangers involved in cigarette smoking. In the first version, the author used the report to argue that manufacturers shouldn't have produced cigarettes; in the second, it's used to argue that people shouldn't have bought cigarettes. Can this evidence be used for such completely different purposes? The answer is 'yes, it can'.

The 1962 report does support both arguments in that, if the knowledge about the effects of smoking were well-known, then we can argue that both manufacturers and smokers were at fault for ignoring this information. Thus this evidence is a good example of how one can provide more than one significance for it. In consequence, an argument which was based on no more than such a piece of evidence is weakened by our being able to show the other significance.

What about some of the other reasoning used? In version 1, we find the claim that 'smoking is addictive', whereas in version 2 we find 'Nobody is forced to either start or, having started, to continue. Furthermore, half of all smokers manage to give up smoking.' Does the evidence in the second version overwhelm the evidence in the first? Or does that in the first significantly weaken the significance of that in the second? They both have the effect of weakening each other, and provide good examples of how one can think of responses to evidence.

Checking analogies

What about the analogies used in the second version? Do they work? Can you think of any analogies that would work for the first version?

Thinking of further reasoning

Can you think of further reasoning for both versions? In addition, can you think of how you could extend the conclusions of each version into a further argument? For example, there has been a suggestion that people who smoke shouldn't be given free health care on the grounds that they knowingly caused their ill-health. How does this fit with version 2? What about the argument that people who are damaged in some way after having taken a medical drug should be able to make a claim against the manufacturer of the drug? How does this fit with version 1? What about illegal drugs?

Rehearsing different scenarios

As you can see, the evaluation of arguments is essentially an imaginative enterprise. All the time, you are coming up with different possibilities, rehearsing different scenarios, looking at alternative lines of reasoning, and seeing where small changes to the reasoning might lead. This imaginative quality should also be applied to your own work. Use the same questioning approach.

Asking evaluative questions

- Looking at the evidence that you have collected, what conclusion can it support?

- What further evidence is needed to produce a stronger conclusion?

- What assumptions do you have to make about the significance of the evidence you're using?

- If you know the sort of conclusion you want to be able to draw, what sort of evidence do you need which would do that?

- What possible counter-arguments can you think of which would seriously threaten your argument?

● How can you weaken these counter-arguments?

Ordering your material

As you now will see, by its emphasis on the rehearsal of alternative scenarios (what if things were different . . ?), critical thinking encourages imagination in your work. But it encourages something else as well: the good ordering of your material. By focusing your attention on the nature of argument, it requires you to have regard to the sequence of your material. Again certain questions need to be asked. The main question, however, is a simple one:

● What is the best sequence of reasoning for your material?

This question includes a number of sub-questions:

(a) Does the reasoning build up its case in an effective sequence, each part adding something which is not already established?

(b) If there are intermediate conclusions, do they fit as a useful sequence heading towards the main conclusion?

(c) Is there a more effective way of presenting the argument, such that some parts should be expanded and others contracted?

(d) As you read through what you have written, can you see that what you are trying to argue – what you are trying to show or prove – is actually argued for. Does it read in a convincing way?

Being a critical thinker doesn't just mean being able to identify the strengths and weaknesses in other's arguments; it also means being able to produce greater strengths and avoid weaknesses in your own. If you can do both, you have learned to swim not only on the bedroom carpet but also in the imaginative possibilities of any ocean.

Glossary

The purpose of this book is to encourage you to use skills of critical thinking rather than requiring you to master the terminology which is used in describing and analysing arguments. Being able to use the skills involved is much more useful than being able to recite terms without using what they refer to. However, some terminology is used in this book, including all of the following.

Ad hominem. A type of argument in which a counter-argument is attacked by criticising some feature or features of the author of this counter-argument (rather than the argument itself).

Analogy. That part of an argument in which two things are compared, on the assumption that if they are similar in one respect they are also similar in a further, relevant way.

Argument. This consists of at least one reason and one conclusion, whose purpose together is to persuade others of the argument's truth.

Assumption. Part of an argument which acts as part of the reasoning, but which is unstated.

Conclusion. That part of an argument which is supported by reasoning. The general point of an argument will be the main conclusion; on the way to drawing a main conclusion, there might be intermediate conclusions drawn.

Deductive argument. A form of argument in which the reasons given for the conclusion are presented in such a way that, if they are true, then so too must be the conclusion.

Inductive argument. A form of argument in which the reasons given for the conclusion are meant to increase the probability of the conclusion being true.

Post hoc. A type of argument in which because one thing follows something else, it is assumed that the latter caused the former.

Reason. A statement which contains a claim of some sort – including evidence and judgements – which is used to support a conclusion.

Tu quoque. A type of argument which tries to show that something of which the arguer is accused cannot be used against them in that others are guilty of the same thing.

Further Reading

There are many books on critical thinking, but a very high proportion of these are more advanced that most students will need. This book has introduced you to a number of techniques that you will find useful in both your reading and writing. If you want further books that will help you in more detail to deal with the type of arguments that you are likely to meet in your studies, then the following can be recommended.

Building Arguments, Drew Hinderer (Wadsworth Publishing). This is expensive, even in paperback, but it is worth the high price, being written in a very approachable way, including the use of illustrations and cartoons (especially Peanuts). One of its great virtues is that it looks at the task of writing critically as well as that of reading in this way. Another is that it looks at some of the big issues, such as animal rights and abortion.

Critical Thinking, William Hughes (Broadview). A comprehensive introduction to the subject written in a way that most students would find straightforward. Running to over 300 pages it clearly covers far more material than we have been able to do, including aspects such as meaning and truth. Lots of self-testing exercises, and some useful advice on writing argumentative essays.

Critical Reasoning, Anne Thomson (Routledge). A very useful guide to a number of critical thinking issues written by someone who is very experienced in both teaching and assessing students in the subject. It is illustrated by using a wide range of the sort of arguments that you find in newspapers and magazines.

Index

Going to University
How to prepare yourself for all aspects of student life

Dennis Farrington

Are you an A-Level student? Are you planning to apply for a place at university? 'Going to university' is something which over 300,000 people do each year, committing several years of their lives and a fair amount of money in the process. If you are planning to join them, this book is a guide through the increasingly complex maze of choices in higher education. It will show you how to get the best from the system, how to choose what is most appropriate, how to satisfy yourself about quality, how to decide where to live, how to get good advice about a career, and many other topics. Follow the expert advice in this book, and make sure you make the right choices at this important stage of your career. You may not get a second chance. Dr Dennis Farrington has worked in senior positions in university administration since 1981. He is a leading authority on the institution-student relationship and the way universities work.

160pp. illus. 1 85703 405 8.

How to Write an Assignment
Improving your research and presentation skills

Pauline Smith

Assignments play a large and increasingly valuable role in studying and learning in further and higher education. Written by an experienced tutor/lecturer, this book offers the student a clear framework for his or her own assignment-based work, and encouraging the development of such skills as information gathering, evidence evaluation, argument and presentation, which will prove valuable not only on educational courses, but in the wider workplace beyond. An experienced teacher, chief examiner and Open University tutor, Pauline Smith now lectures at Manchester Metropolitan University.

108pp. illus. 1 85703 210 1. 2nd edition.

How to Pass Exams Without Anxiety
Every candidate's guide to success

David Acres

Now in its fourth and fully revised edition this is the best all-round exams handbook available for students on the market today. 'Must be high on the list of essential reading for all those involved in the matter of taking examinations . . . Written in crisp concise style with the text clearly laid out.' *Comlon (LCCI).* 'A specialist in study skills and techniques gives expert guidance.' *Teacher's Weekly.* 'Gives some very sensible advice.' *Focus on Business Education.* 'A thorough survey . . . easy to use, with checklists, summaries, reference headings and cartoons.' *Times Educational Supplement.* 'Good advice on revision and anxiety management.' *National Extension College.* 'Highly recommended.' *Open University.* David Acres is Learning Support Tutor at the College of St. Mark & St. John, Plymouth, and a specialist in study skills training and development.

168pp. illus. 1 85703 174 1. 4th edition.

Studying for a Degree
How to succeed as a mature student in higher education

Stephen Wade

If you are an aspiring student in adult education, or a mature learner looking for a higher education course leading to a degree, this book is specially for you. It will lead you through the academic maze of entry procedures, study programmes and teaching methods. It explains how to apply and how to contact the professionals who will help; how to survive tutorials, seminars and presentations, and how to manage your time, plan your study, and find the right support when you need it. There are sections on the credit award system, pathway planning, and useful case studies of typical students in this context. Stephen Wade PhD has 20 years' professional experience in further and higher education, and is a Course Leader for a degree programme.

160pp. illus. 1 85703 415 5.

Writing an Essay
Winning techniques and skills for students

Brendan Hennessy

Now in its third edition, this popular book will be an invaluable help to all students faced with writing essays, whether at school, college or university. Written by an experienced writing skills consultant and lecturer, it explains the different approaches and techniques needed for essays in the humanities, social sciences and other disciplines. With the aid of examples, case studies and practical exercises, it discusses step-by-step how to choose the topic, how to research it, think about it, take notes, plan and compose the finished essay. The author also demonstrates how organising information, and using it to present coherent arguments and conclusions can be just as valuable in business, as in an educational setting. 'There is much good sense in this book.' *Times Educational Supplement.* 'If you're a student, buy it.' *Writers Monthly.*

176pp. illus. 1 85703 159 8. 3rd edition.

How to Master Languages
For business, study, travel and living abroad

Roger Jones

With the expansion of international contacts and the advent of the global market, languages are more valuable than ever before. Written for business people, students and others, this book discusses: why learn a language, which language to choose, language training and where to find it, getting down to language learning, children and languages, and language training in organisations. A large reference section completes the book, giving information on an enormous variety of courses, guides and study material, providing an overview of the world's myriad languages and their use today. 'Full of really practical information and advice, this book will show you how to make the right choices, and add a whole new dimension to your social life, career and business prospects.' *Nexus Expatriate Magazine.* Roger Jones DipTESL is himself an experienced linguist, writer and educational consultant.

160pp. illus. 1 85703 092 3.

How to Study & Learn
Your practical guide to effective study skills

Peter Marshall

Are you thinking of studying or training for an important qualification? Do you know the right techniques for studying and learning, to ensure you achieve the best results as quickly as possible? Whether you are at college or university, doing projects and assignments, writing essays, receiving continuous assessment or preparing for exams, this is the book for you. In practical steps it covers getting your thinking right, organising yourself properly, finding and processing the information you need, reading effectively, developing good writing skills, thinking creatively, motivating yourself, and more. Whatever your subject, age or background, start now – and turn yourself into a winning candidate. Peter Marshall BA BSc (Econ) has a wealth of experience as a university and college teacher.

160pp. illus. 1 85703 062 1.

How to Study Abroad
Your guide to successful planning and decision making

Teresa Tinsley

Studying abroad can open up a whole new horizon of opportunities, but what courses are available? How does one qualify? What does it cost? Can anyone do it? Now in a fully updated third edition, this book brings together a wealth of fascinating advice and reference information. It covers what to study (everything from short study visits to postgraduate opportunities), getting a place, entrance requirements, when and how to apply, grants and scholarships, helpful agencies and contacts, validation of courses, what to expect (teaching, services), financing your stay, accommodation, fitting in, travel and visas, health and insurance and more, and complete with a country-by-country guide. 'The book is straightforward to use, with a good index, lists all the main reference sources likely to be found in a careers library, and is just the thing to provide a quick answer to those difficult questions.' *Phoenix/Association of Graduate Careers Advisory Services.* Teresa Tinsley BA DipEd MIL is Conferences Organiser at CILT, the Centre for Information on Language Teaching.

176pp. illus. 1 85703 169 5. 3rd edition.

How To Books provide practical help on a large range of topics. They are available through all good bookshops or can be ordered direct from the distributors. Just tick the titles you want and complete the form on the following page.

___ Apply to an Industrial Tribunal (£7.99)
___ Applying for a Job (£7.99)
___ Applying for a United States Visa (£15.99)
___ Be a Freelance Journalist (£8.99)
___ Be a Freelance Secretary (£8.99)
___ Be a Local Councillor (£8.99)
___ Be an Effective School Governor (£9.99)
___ Become a Freelance Sales Agent (£9.99)
___ Become an Au Pair (£8.99)
___ Buy & Run a Shop (£8.99)
___ Buy & Run a Small Hotel (£8.99)
___ Cash from your Computer (£9.99)
___ Career Planning for Women (£8.99)
___ Choosing a Nursing Home (£8.99)
___ Claim State Benefits (£9.99)
___ Communicate at Work (£7.99)
___ Conduct Staff Appraisals (£7.99)
___ Conducting Effective Interviews (£8.99)
___ Copyright & Law for Writers (£8.99)
___ Counsel People at Work (£7.99)
___ Creating a Twist in the Tale (£8.99)
___ Creative Writing (£9.99)
___ Critical Thinking for Students (£8.99)
___ Do Voluntary Work Abroad (£8.99)
___ Do Your Own Advertising (£8.99)
___ Do Your Own PR (£8.99)
___ Doing Business Abroad (£9.99)
___ Emigrate (£9.99)
___ Employ & Manage Staff (£8.99)
___ Find Temporary Work Abroad (£8.99)
___ Finding a Job in Canada (£9.99)
___ Finding a Job in Computers (£8.99)
___ Finding a Job in New Zealand (£9.99)
___ Finding a Job with a Future (£8.99)
___ Finding Work Overseas (£9.99)
___ Freelance DJ-ing (£8.99)
___ Get a Job Abroad (£10.99)
___ Get a Job in America (£9.99)
___ Get a Job in Australia (£9.99)
___ Get a Job in Europe (£9.99)
___ Get a Job in France (£9.99)
___ Get a Job in Germany (£9.99)
___ Get a Job in Hotels and Catering (£8.99)
___ Get a Job in Travel & Tourism (£8.99)
___ Get into Films & TV (£8.99)
___ Get into Radio (£8.99)
___ Get That Job (£6.99)
___ Getting your First Job (£8.99)
___ Going to University (£8.99)
___ Helping your Child to Read (£8.99)
___ Investing in People (£8.99)
___ Invest in Stocks & Shares (£8.99)

___ Keep Business Accounts (£7.99)
___ Know Your Rights at Work (£8.99)
___ Know Your Rights: Teachers (£6.99)
___ Live & Work in America (£9.99)
___ Live & Work in Australia (£12.99)
___ Live & Work in Germany (£9.99)
___ Live & Work in Greece (£9.99)
___ Live & Work in Italy (£8.99)
___ Live & Work in New Zealand (£9.99)
___ Live & Work in Portugal (£9.99)
___ Live & Work in Spain (£7.99)
___ Live & Work in the Gulf (£9.99)
___ Living & Working in Britain (£8.99)
___ Living & Working in China (£9.99)
___ Living & Working in Hong Kong (£10.99)
___ Living & Working in Israel (£10.99)
___ Living & Working in Japan (£8.99)
___ Living & Working in Saudi Arabia (£12.99)
___ Living & Working in the Netherlands (£9.99)
___ Lose Weight & Keep Fit (£6.99)
___ Make a Wedding Speech (£7.99)
___ Making a Complaint (£8.99)
___ Manage a Sales Team (£8.99)
___ Manage an Office (£8.99)
___ Manage Computers at Work (£8.99)
___ Manage People at Work (£8.99)
___ Manage Your Career (£8.99)
___ Managing Budgets & Cash Flows (£9.99)
___ Managing Meetings (£8.99)
___ Managing Your Personal Finances (£8.99)
___ Market Yourself (£8.99)
___ Master Book-Keeping (£8.99)
___ Mastering Business English (£8.99)
___ Master GCSE Accounts (£8.99)
___ Master Languages (£8.99)
___ Master Public Speaking (£8.99)
___ Obtaining Visas & Work Permits (£9.99)
___ Organising Effective Training (£9.99)
___ Pass Exams Without Anxiety (£7.99)
___ Pass That Interview (£6.99)
___ Plan a Wedding (£7.99)
___ Prepare a Business Plan (£8.99)
___ Publish a Book (£9.99)
___ Publish a Newsletter (£9.99)
___ Raise Funds & Sponsorship (£7.99)
___ Rent & Buy Property in France (£9.99)
___ Rent & Buy Property in Italy (£9.99)
___ Retire Abroad (£8.99)
___ Return to Work (£7.99)
___ Run a Local Campaign (£6.99)
___ Run a Voluntary Group (£8.99)
___ Sell Your Business (£9.99)

___ Selling into Japan (£14.99)	___ Use the Internet (£9.99)
___ Setting up Home in Florida (£9.99)	___ Winning Consumer Competitions (£8.99)
___ Spend a Year Abroad (£8.99)	___ Winning Presentations (£8.99)
___ Start a Business from Home (£7.99)	___ Work from Home (£8.99)
___ Start a New Career (£6.99)	___ Work in an Office (£7.99)
___ Starting to Manage (£8.99)	___ Work in Retail (£8.99)
___ Starting to Write (£8.99)	___ Work with Dogs (£8.99)
___ Start Word Processing (£8.99)	___ Working Abroad (£14.99)
___ Start Your Own Business (£8.99)	___ Working as a Holiday Rep (£9.99)
___ Study Abroad (£8.99)	___ Working in Japan (£10.99)
___ Study & Learn (£7.99)	___ Working in Photography (£8.99)
___ Study & Live in Britain (£7.99)	___ Working in the Gulf (£10.99)
___ Studying at University (£8.99)	___ Working on Contract Worldwide (£9.99)
___ Studying for a Degree (£8.99)	___ Working on Cruise Ships (£9.99)
___ Successful Grandparenting (£8.99)	___ Write a CV that Works (£7.99)
___ Successful Mail Order Marketing (£9.99)	___ Write a Press Release (£9.99)
___ Successful Single Parenting (£8.99)	___ Write a Report (£8.99)
___ Survive at College (£4.99)	___ Write an Assignment (£8.99)
___ Survive Divorce (£8.99)	___ Write an Essay (£7.99)
___ Surviving Redundancy (£8.99)	___ Write & Sell Computer Software (£9.99)
___ Take Care of Your Heart (£5.99)	___ Write Business Letters (£8.99)
___ Taking in Students (£8.99)	___ Write for Publication (£8.99)
___ Taking on Staff (£8.99)	___ Write for Television (£8.99)
___ Taking Your A-Levels (£8.99)	___ Write Your Dissertation (£8.99)
___ Teach Abroad (£8.99)	___ Writing a Non Fiction Book (£8.99)
___ Teach Adults (£8.99)	___ Writing & Selling a Novel (£8.99)
___ Teaching Someone to Drive (£8.99)	___ Writing & Selling Short Stories (£8.99)
___ Travel Round the World (£8.99)	___ Writing Reviews (£8.99)
___ Use a Library (£6.99)	___ Your Own Business in Europe (£12.99)

To: Plymbridge Distributors Ltd, Plymbridge House, Estover Road, Plymouth PL6 7PZ. Customer Services Tel: (01752) 202301. Fax: (01752) 202331.

Please send me copies of the titles I have indicated. Please add postage & packing (UK £1, Europe including Eire, £2, World £3 airmail).

☐ I enclose cheque/PO payable to Plymbridge Distributors Ltd for £ [   ]

☐ Please charge to my ☐ MasterCard, ☐ Visa, ☐ AMEX card.

Account No. [   ]

Card Expiry Date [ ] 19 [ ]   ☎ Credit Card orders may be faxed or phoned.

Customer Name (CAPITALS) ....

Address ....

.... Postcode...............

Telephone........................... Signature ....

Every effort will be made to despatch your copy as soon as possible but to avoid possible disappointment please allow up to 21 days for despatch time (42 days if overseas). Prices and availability are subject to change without notice.

[Code BPA]